Tales From Out Yonder

Ross McSwain

Republic of Texas Press
Plano, Texas

Library of Congress Cataloging-in-Publication Data

McSwain, Ross.
    Tales from out yonder / Ross McSwain.
        p.   cm.
    Includes bibliographical references and index.
    ISBN 1-55622-848-1 (pbk.)
    1. Texas, West--Description and travel--Anecdotes.   2. Texas,
    West--History, Local--Anecdotes.   3. Texas, West--
    Biography--Anecdotes.   I. Title.

F386.6 ,T35 2001
976.4'06—dc21   2001019724

Republic of Texas Press is an imprint of Wordware Publishing, Inc.
No part of this book may be reproduced in any form or by
any means without permission in writing from
Wordware Publishing, Inc.

Printed in the United States of America

ISBN 1-55622-848-1
10 9 8 7 6 5 4 3 2 1
0106

All inquiries for volume purchases of this book should be addressed to
Wordware Publishing, Inc., at 2320 Los Rios Boulevard, Plano, Texas 75074.
Telephone inquiries may be made by calling:
(972) 423-0090

Tales From Out Yonder

Contents

Part I—People

Contents

Part II—Places

Part III—Things

Contents

Look Yonder

To our friend Ross McSwain:

We are pleased that you have published this book; another work in your phase of writing and storytelling that probes down into the roots of human life and existence concerning the past of this world we grew up in and that we hold dear to our souls.

Recently, Ross and I traveled together across a span of miles that covered portions of the very heartland of our beloved arid, semiarid, and desert-home region.

On this vast acreage the proliferation of communication towers, wind-power generators, and electronic petroleum recovery devices continues to accelerate. We are leaving our past at an alarming rate. The speed of dispatch has grown even now to a point that we are obsolete in many areas before a product reaches the consumer market.

Now comes Ross. I can envision this gifted writer standing on the highest peak of the region and casting his eyes to the north, south, east, and west, boxing every degree of the compass and noting what has taken place and what is happening now across Our Land.

Ross will not let us forget where we live, who we live with, where we have been, where we are now, and a bit on where we will go. With his well-read "Out Yonder" series of articles and books he continues to give us exceptional insight into both "back yonder" and "in the yonder," based on the Land and the People.

His knowledge of the Land covered in his work and of the People that constitute its inhabitants is beyond that of any one person coming out this way from the beginning of history as we know it. He has made a life-study of the Soil and the Seed Stock that was used in creation of this unique geographical setting.

Innovative, insightful, sometimes joyous, sometimes melancholy is the essence of the "Out Yonder" series.

Fascinating descriptions of the Land and vivid accounts of the People through the good times and through devastating storms will not let the world forget where we are and who we are.

From the early-times era — from the trailblazing homesteaders, range wars, family feuds — from hot volcanic ash to shoulder-high grazing grass — from our constant battle now against thorn-cactus, cedar, mequite, and low water levels — we live here and we love it.

Ross, thank you for keeping us on this very interesting and well-trodden trail until we all go to our True Home with our Lord and Savior.

Jerry Mack Johnson
San Angelo, Texas
February 2001

Author's note: My friend, Jerry Mack Johnson, author of seven books, including *Country Wisdom*, published in 1974 by Doubleday, a Pulitzer nominee, died on May 14, 2001, in a San Angelo, Texas hospital after a long illness. I will miss him very much.

Preface

In 1979 while working as regional editor of the *San Angelo (Texas) Standard-Times,* the editor suggested that I write an occasional column about people, places, or things that I found interesting as I traveled the fifty-four counties of Southwestern Texas, the Hill Country, and the remote reaches of the Big Bend. This area was about the size of the state of Pennsylvania, although it certainly did not have the same population.

Like most newspaper reporters who come into contact with large numbers of people, my notebooks were filled with various kinds of information that was never used. A general interest column would be an ideal way to use more story material, utilize more names of people, and perhaps include more regional community activities in the newspaper.

In the beginning the column would have two or more items. As time passed, a single subject became more acceptable to the editors. Photographs were generally used to illustrate each column, but it was not a mandatory requirement simply because photos of some subjects were not available.

The column name, *"Out Yonder,"* came about by accident. My late friend Dave Smith, then serving as the newspaper's city editor, had to answer my telephone when I was away from the office.

"Hello, McSwain's desk," Smith would say.

"Where is he? When will he be back? Who the hell knows? He's Out Yonder someplace!"

I will always be indebted to Dave Smith for coming up with that wonderful title for the column, which will soon be twenty-two years old.

This is the third volume of stories gleaned from column materials. Much of the material in this book is new. However, some of the material originally appearing in columns has been rewritten and updated. Previously published material is used with the permission of the *San Angelo Standard-Times.*

The book is divided into three sections: People, Places, and Things. Subjects range from persons and incidents of the past to more modern day happenings. Things cover all sorts of subjects, ranging from old homes to Indian pictographs and from a wild and woolly land rush to finding a madstone to cure "hydraphoby."

Western Texas has been my beat for more than a quarter-century. I have covered every kind of news story, from the trials and tribulations of con man Billie Sol Estes to the Sanderson flood and the Cayanosa tornado, which collectively killed more than fifty people. I believe I also attended the longest lasting school board meeting ever held, if such a record is posted in the Guinness Book. The meeting started at eight o'clock in the evening and was finally over about four o'clock in the morning. It was a hard decision for the board members that night to fire the school superintendent at Terlingua.

Acknowledgments

The publication of *Tales from Out Yonder,* the third volume of stories that I have written since 1988, was made possible because of the support and work of several persons. Special thanks go to Jack Pate, publisher, and Perry Flippin, editor, *San Angelo Standard-Times*, for granting permission to use certain material and photographs that originally appeared in the Out Yonder column. Also, to my longtime friends and mentors, Elmer Kelton and Jerry Mack Johnson, a special thank you for their longtime support. Both of these men are award-winning authors and Pulitzer prize nominees who have provided me with encouragement over several decades of writing and reporting.

Also, special thanks go to Jo-Ann Palmer of Sonora, secretary of the Sutton County Historical Society; Frederica Burt Wyatt of Junction, secretary of the Kimble County Historical Society; Margaret Waring of Comanche, who is in charge of the county library there; Angela Way, curator of the Big Spring Heritage Museum; Lorene Bishop, Brown County Historical Society; Jane Hoerster, Mason County Historical Society; Bill Porter, Menard County Historical Society; Dan Feather, editor and publisher, *Menard News;* Edna Sedeno, librarian and archivist of the *San Angelo Standard-Times*; Felton Cochran of San Angelo, owner of the Cactus Book Shop; Suzanne Campbell of San Angelo, head of the Dr. Ralph P. Chase West Texas Collection at Angelo State University's Porter Henderson Memorial Library, and her assistant, Tanya Norris, for help in research and collecting photographs.

Also, I want to extend special thanks to my Republic of Texas Press editor, Ginnie Bivona, for encouraging me to produce this third volume, and to many others who have expressed interest in seeing that these stories are saved for future Texans.

I'll be seeing you Out Yonder.

Ross McSwain
San Angelo, Texas

Part I
People

Eloping Lovers' Story Ends Violently

RUNNING AWAY TO GET MAR-RIED, or eloping, is nothing unusual in these days and times. In fact, fathers most likely would be better off financially if their daughters chose to just take off with the man of their dreams and get hitched by a justice of the peace or friendly retired minister.

A modern wedding, despite the work of financial planners, can cost huge sums of money, with wedding dresses alone bringing upwards to $1,000 or more. Add cakes, flowers, attendants, and a zillion other details and the cost can put a serious dent in the family retirement fund.

Eloping to Las Vegas or Hawaii or to some place in the Caribbean can bring on all sorts of romantic thoughts. A lot of couples will choose to do that, hopefully with the blessing of Mom, Dad, and all the kinfolks.

Eloping, however, in days past could get a couple in very serious trouble. In fact, one eloping couple from Central Texas died violently in a gun duel south of Sonora in 1921 when the girl's father, mother, and brother hunted the lovers down after a 400-mile chase across Texas. Most everyone except the intended bride was toting a pistol, including Mom.

According to a story that appeared in the May 23, 1921 edition of the *San Angelo Standard-Times*, Elizabeth Dorothy Harris, 20, of Valley Mills, a community near Waco, was killed and her fiancé, Nelson McNeill, 27, was seriously wounded when the pair was overtaken in an automobile chase by the young woman's father and mother, Mr. and Mrs. Dick Harris, and her brother, Harry Sim Harris, all of Valley Mills.

The headlines in the newspaper for several days spoke volumes about the incident: "Girl Killed As Fiance and Her Father Battle – Four Hundred Mile Chase After Elopers Ends, Duel Ensues." The newspaper followed the story until its conclusion.

The chase ended near the Joe Wyatt pasture about eleven miles southeast of Sonora at four o'clock on Saturday afternoon.

When the girl's fiancé, McNeill, and her father started to shoot at each other, the girl was caught in between them, pleading with them not to do anything drastic.

Sutton County Sheriff B. W. Hutcherson of Sonora told reporters that the people were heavily armed with four pistols and a shotgun. Hutcherson led a 30-man search party that evening in an effort to locate the wounded McNeill, but the search was called off about three o'clock in the morning when the searchers lost track of the blood trail. The young Harris woman died from gunshot wounds to the chest, stomach, and face.

The woman's fiancé, McNeill, was found dead the next day in the Steen pasture about seven miles from the gun battle site. His throat had been slashed and a bloody penknife was found near the body. He also had several bullet wounds in his body, and the second finger on his right hand had been almost shot off. The wound appeared to have been made by a load of buckshot.

When Justice of the Peace H. B. Balch conducted an inquiry into McNeill's death, it was believed that the wounded man had slashed

Above: *Dorothy Harris in swimming costume, circa 1920.* Above right: *Mr. and Mrs. Dick Harris, fourth and fifth from left, are shown outside the McDonald Hotel in Sonora, Texas, the next day after the shooting. Standing at far right is their son, Harry Sims Harris, who also took part in the gunfight. Photos courtesy Sutton County Historical Society.*

his own throat using his left hand.

"A ragged slash across the

throat was the only perceptible wound on McNeill's body which would have been fatal," a report stated.

The Harris father and son were charged with assault with intent to murder and both were released on $1,000 bond.

In an interview, the dead woman's white-haired father said that McNeill and his daughter had been sweethearts for some time, but the family objected to McNeill's attentions because he did not have any business (or was simply unemployed). The Harris and McNeill families were well known in Bosque County. Nelson

McNeill was the son of Dr. W. T. McNeill, one of Valley Mills' physicians.

According to the interview given by the father, the chase began when the daughter failed to return home from a trip to Waco on the previous Sunday, May 14, 1921. The parents went to Waco to find her but while there, received word that she had gone to Dallas and was in good health. When the parents reached Dallas, they learned that the telegram they had received from the daughter was false, apparently sent by a friend of McNeill to throw the parents off in their search for the couple.

In another newspaper article published on May 23, 1921, it was reported that McNeill was known to make frequent trips to the Del Rio area where he liked to hunt and fish, so the Harris family left Waco on Friday, May 19, 1921, and headed for Sonora and Del Rio.

While the woman's father was making inquiries about the couple and giving a description of the Buick roadster they were in, McNeill and his sweetheart drove down Main Street, right past the enraged father. The chase was on.

When McNeill was about eleven miles from town, a wheel on his car collapsed and his Buick roadster ran into a ditch. He had driven on the rim for miles after blowing out a tire on the dirt road. The Harris family—father, mother, and son—were close behind in a Hudson Super 6, one of the faster automobiles of the time.

Harris told lawmen that when he jumped out of his car with his shotgun, McNeill shot at him first with a pistol. The son, armed with a .45-caliber six-shooter, tried to flank the couple, who were hiding behind some bushes.

H. S. Harris told law officers that his sister started toward her parents when they called to her, but that McNeill reached out to stop her. Three shots were fired, and the girl fell dead.

Officers found bullet casings scattered all over the area, and four pistols and a shotgun were recovered. Each of the Harris family was armed, as well as McNeill.

A coroner's report ruled that Miss Harris had been killed by a person or persons unknown. Nelson McNeill's death was ruled a suicide. The assault charges brought against Harris and his son were eventually dropped, and the McNeill family made no effort to prosecute the Harrises in connection with the case.

A telegram sent as a ruse apparently triggered the 400-mile chase. The dead girl's father, Dick Harris, related details of the chase and the shooting a short while after arriving in Sonora from the remote ranch where the gun duel took place.

"My daughter left our home in Valley Mills a week ago Saturday, saying that she would spend the day with a friend in Waco. That afternoon she did not return. Her mother and I were uneasy. We called to see why she did not return, and found that she had not been with the friend she had said she would go visit," the father told news reporters.

"The next day we went to Waco. Monday we received a telegram from Dallas signed by her saying that she was there and that everything was all right and that she was writing that day. The telegram stated she was with a girlfriend there.

"We could not wait for the letter," the father said. "We went to Dallas to see that she was all right. In Dallas we found that she had not been there—that a telegram had been sent from San Antonio, telling another person in Dallas to send the telegram we received, signing her name to it."

Harris and his wife, both haggard but showing little sign of emotion or nervousness, continued their explanation of the chase that ended so tragically.

"A little later we learned that McNeill had left town on Saturday morning. We found that he had told at the garage that his car would be gone for some time as he was going to Dallas. Then we started the search for her. We have visited every county seat and every courthouse in the surrounding counties. For a week we have followed close behind, but always far enough behind to fail to meet them.

"In Sonora," father Harris said, "we were explaining to the landlady about the people we were looking for when they came into town. The race followed. Their car broke down and they made for cover in the brush along the road. I jumped from the car and called to my daughter that she'd better come back or to lie down or she would get killed. Mrs. Harris was calling to her, too, and my son was making toward them from the side.

"My daughter hesitated a moment and turned to go toward her mother when McNeill took her by the wrist, turned her around, and keeping her between me and him, backed behind some bushes," the father continued. "Instantly my son yelled, 'he's shooting her, he's shooting her,'

> Officers found bullet casings scattered all over the area, and four pistols and a shotgun were recovered. Each of the Harris family was armed, as well as McNeill.

and he did. Then he turned the gun on himself. I did not see this but my son did," Harris told reporters.

According to the news report, Harris said he did not care to talk about what happened after he and his son closed in on McNeill. He said he would tell that part of the story later if he had to, but he refused to make any other statement and said that his son or wife would have nothing to say. Harris was described as being about sixty years old with a heavy shock of white hair. Mrs. Harris, a delicate-looking woman, showed the strain of the past week, reporters noted.

The Harris family spent most of that Sunday evening and night in Sonora. The men quickly made bond, signed by a number of prominent Sonora citizens, and then they were escorted to San Angelo where their daughter's body had been taken to an undertaking establishment. The mother and father accompanied the body home by train while the son drove the family car to Valley Mills.

The body of Nelson McNeill also was shipped to Valley Mills by Santa Fe train. A Doctor Goodall, of Waco, a close family friend of the McNeills, had come to San Angelo to bring the body back for the ailing father, Dr. W. T. McNeill. Meanwhile, several McNeill relatives, including his uncle, A. A. McNeill, cousins James A. and A. A. McNeill Jr., and C. E. Scrutchfrield, arrived in Sonora. The McNeills announced that so far as they were concerned there would be no private prosecution of the charges against Harris and his son. However, that matter would rest with Dr. W. T. McNeill, father of the dead man, and Dr. Goodall who had examined the bodies and gathered other information. The McNeill relatives noted to reporters that they were of the opinion that Dr. McNeill would not press the charges with private prosecution.

While in Sonora, the McNeills identified one of the weapons found at the shooting scene as a .32-caliber automatic pistol, which Nelson McNeill had borrowed from his uncle sometime before leaving Valley Mills.

Investigating officials said an arsenal of weapons were involved. Another .32-caliber pistol was identified as belonging to the dead woman's mother. It was found in the Harris auto and had not been fired. A .38-caliber pistol, which officers said belonged to the father, Dick Harris, also had not been fired. Harris admitted shooting at McNeill with a 12-gauge shotgun loaded with buckshot. It was found in the Harris automobile at the shooting site with a smashed stock. Another shotgun was found in McNeill's automobile. It was a 16-gauge shotgun loaded with birdshot and had not been fired.

Several physicians, appointed by the coroner, conducted an examination of the bodies of both Miss Harris and her fiancé, McNeill. Three bullets had entered her body, all of them passing through the body except for one which crashed into the right side of her neck, breaking her neck and lodging in her left cheek. The bullet removed was a .32-caliber steel jacketed bullet. The doctors also noted that buckshot also would cause a wound similar to that caused by a .32-caliber bullet.

McNeill's wounds included the jagged cut across the throat, a seriously mangled hand that had a finger nearly blown off from a shotgun projectile, and a glancing wound in the forehead that would not have been fatal. The head wound was believed to have been caused by a glancing blow from Harris' shotgun, which he tried to use as a club. The man's son later told authorities that he had disarmed his father to keep him from killing McNeill while he was down.

The violent gunfight between the girl's family and her fiancé drew statewide attention, with newspapers carrying lengthy stories of the gun duel, their burial, and comments from their individual friends.

The tragic death of the couple drew comments from friends of McNeill and his girlfriend. The news of their deaths on May 21, 1921, came as a terrible shock to his friends in Del Rio, one newspaper story stated.

"During the past year, McNeill was a frequent visitor to this town. He was an enthusiastic hunter and fisherman, and it was to indulge his love of these sports that he came here so often."

However, some believed that McNeill was smuggling in Mexican liquor and hauling it to Central Texas and selling it.

"Handsome, courteous, and always in a happy mood, he fascinated all who knew him. While here, he spent his evenings at the Elks Club where his gentle manners made him a favorite," the news story said.

"Accompanied by Miss Harris, Nelson McNeill paid his last visit to Del Rio on Monday, May 16. The couple stopped at the Gray Hotel where they occupied separate rooms and registered separately. During the evening McNeill received several telegrams. He told friends that they were from his fiancée's father and that they were of a threatening nature. Next morning (Tuesday) the couple left early for Sonora. McNeill stated they were bound for Valley Mills, the home of both.

"Nothing else was heard from them until 6:30 p.m. on Saturday when Val Verde County Sheriff Bud Whistler received a long distance message from the Sutton County sheriff that told Whistler that the dead body of Miss Harris had been found beside an automobile on the road to the Joe Wyatt Ranch. McNeill had disappeared," the news report related. The Sutton sheriff suspected that McNeill had killed the girl and that he was trying to escape, and he asked Whistler to watch all trains bound east since it was possible that McNeill might reach Comstock and board a train there.

My friend and fellow history lover Jo-Ann Palmer has been intrigued by this story for years. I learned about the details from Mrs. Palmer, who was kind enough to share her research into the matter.

Why had the Harrises been so concerned about their daughter's involvement with McNeill? He was from a well-to-do family in Valley Mills, had served as a medic in World War I, and had nearly completed medical school at Vanderbilt University before he joined the Army in 1917. The Harrises had expressed concern earlier that McNeill had no business and apparently was unemployed. However, he had adequate funds to travel, to spend time hunting and fishing, and to pursue other pleasures, thus he was suspected by the girl's father as being a bootlegger.

The girl's father told news reporters after the fracas was over that "I objected to my daughter's associating with McNeill because of his character and she and her mother had many arguments about him. She would reply that he was not as bad as they said he was and that _elop

other girls of the best families in Valley Mills went with him."

In 1991 Mrs. Palmer wrote Jane Schinzinger in Irvine, California, and provided the woman copies of some of the clippings concerning the shooting. Mrs. Schinzinger is the daughter of the late Harry Sim Harris, the son involved in the duel and brother of the dead woman.

"When I was a child I thought that I had an aunt (Dorothy Harris) who had died of tuberculosis. My parents moved to California about 1925. I don't believe that I met my grandmother until we visited Texas about 1947. At that time she mentioned to my father in my hearing that she had made a scrapbook of newspaper accounts ... and that there were many things wrong. She and my grandfather (Dick Harris) evidently believed that Dorothy was being taken to Mexico to be sold into White Slavery. My father got tears in his eyes and said, 'I don't want to discuss it.' And he never did. My mother also said little, even after his death," Mrs. Schinzinger wrote.

"The shooting had a profound effect on him and on the way my sister and I were raised," Mrs. Schinzinger added. "His parents had evidently been quite authoritarian. By the time I was in high school and college, he refused to give any advice that might be interpreted as telling us what to do with our lives. We were to make the decisions that affected the directions that our lives took, and we would be responsible for the consequences.

"He had adored his younger sister (Dorothy) and never got over her death and the way it happened. My sister was named Dorothy," Mrs. Schinzinger wrote.

In a footnote to her letter to Mrs. Palmer, the Harris granddaughter stated that her grandfather, Dick Harris, died of a stroke only eight months after the bloody gunfight.

And why wasn't the shooting case prosecuted?

Although there does not appear to be any documented proof, there apparently was an agreement made between the Harris and McNeill families that no charges would be filed and that the McNeill family would make no claim against the estate of Dorothy Harris. Some say that the couple had married in Mexico during the week of their race across the state and that McNeill and his heirs would have a legal claim to any estate of the dead woman since she preceded him in death. Reportedly, the father had ripped rings off his daughter's hand and threw them away at the shooting site. Mrs. Palmer was told by a prominent Sonora rancher that a "band with diamonds" was found along with a number of empty shell casings a number of years later when he and another man, using a metal detector, found the items. At the time the Sonora rancher was managing the property.

"I never got a signed statement from the man before he died," Mrs. Palmer said. Also, in her research she has never uncovered any record of a marriage between McNeill and the Harris woman.

Although both of the lovers were interred in the same cemetery after their untimely death, Dorothy Harris' father had her body removed later to another burial plot at Whitney.

In an effort to get the story of the shooting as complete as possible, Mrs. Palmer also tried to get information from the McNeill family. One relative wrote her in October 1990 that he had seen Nelson McNeill only once and he was dressed in his World War I uniform. He called the man "dapper" looking. Others she contacted were upset and asked that they not be contacted again about the matter, thus a photograph of Nelson McNeill has never been found.

In years past, when the country road was still open to the public, some people around Sonora reported seeing the ghosts of the young couple walking hand in hand along the road just before sunset.

"It's kind of nice to think of them walking forever hand in hand and happy after all they went through," she said.

C. W. Post, the Cereal King

Grape Nuts and other crunchy stuff

FOR OVER 100 YEARS, folks have been crunching away at breakfast time on Grape Nuts, a somewhat tasty cereal that has an appearance like creek gravel.

Grape Nuts and a whole lot of other cereals like Post Bran Flakes and Post Toasties are the creation of C.W. Post, who made a mark in West Texas when few folks knew where the place was located.

Charles William Post was not a Texan by birth. He came to Texas by choice after suffering a nervous breakdown in November 1885 caused by strain and overwork. A native of Springfield, Illinois, Post attended schools there and later attended Illinois Industrial University, now the University of Illinois at Urbana.

At seventeen Post went to Independence, Kansas, where he worked as a salesman, clerk, and store owner. He later returned to Springfield in 1872 and spent the next fourteen years working as a salesman and manufacturer of agricultural machines. During this period he invented and received patents on such farm equipment as cultivators, a sulky plow, a harrow, and a haystacker. He married Ella Letitia Merriweather on November 4, 1874, and the couple had a daughter. However, Post and his wife lived apart for several years, and they divorced in 1904. That same year, he married Leila Young of Battle Creek, Michigan, on November 7.

Post was one of West Texas's first entrepreneurs. After his breakdown, he came to then fledgling Fort Worth in 1886 where he became associated with a group of real estate men who were developing a 300-acre tract in the eastern part of the city in an area now known as Riverside. Other members of the family, including Post's brother, Rollin, followed him to Fort Worth. In 1888 the Posts acquired a 200-acre ranch on the outskirts of the city and began the development of a subdivision on the property; they laid out streets and lots for houses and constructed a woolen mill and a paper mill.

Post suffered another breakdown in 1891. He moved his wife

from Fort Worth to Battle Creek, Michigan, where he entered a sanitarium. With rest and the administrations of a Christian Science practitioner, Post soon was recuperating. The sanitarium, ironically, was owned by a man named Kellogg, who also got into the cereal business.

While being treated at the sanitarium, Post got interested in dietetics. He was convinced that his illness and many others were rooted in people's diets. He was determined to find a health food for the masses.

His first effort at finding a dietetic food came about when he recalled Kansas farmers drinking a substitute for coffee, which was a scarce commodity on the plains. The drink was made of commonly found ingredients and included chicory. Post did not like chicory, so he substituted blackstrap molasses as a sweetener and to provide flavor. In 1885 he introduced his product called "Postum." It was soon an overwhelming success because of Post's genius for marketing.

In 1897 Post introduced his cereal Grape Nuts, and by 1906 most every home in America was using one of his cereal products.

Despite his success as a cereal merchant, Post continued to push himself to greater things. He served as president of the American Manufacturers Association and of the Citizens Industrial Association. He was a bitter opponent of labor unions and was an advocate of the open shop. Then he suffered a third breakdown. Rather than rest and recuperate in Michigan, Post returned to Fort Worth where he was to first learn about western Texas. After visiting the area several times and seeing the potential for farmland development, the cereal magnate bought 213,324 acres of land from the Llano Livestock Company in 1906. He paid $2.25 an acre for the place, which contained nearly 200 square miles of mostly Garza County and spilled over into Hockley County. This was the place where Post would start his most imaginative and philanthropic undertaking.

Post set about building a town on his sprawling acreage, turning some of the lands into farms complete with houses, barns, pens, fencing, water wells, and windmills. The farms sold on the installment plan, one percent down and $62.50 per month for fifteen years. When payoff time came, the farmer would own 160 acres, along with all the improvements. The town also was laid out in a similar manner with houses and businesses ready for buyers to move in. He also set up the town's water system and eventually provided telephone service as well.

Post chose a site near the center of Garza County to be the location of his new town, which also would serve as the county seat. In 1907 Post City, as it was called until after the developer's death, was platted. Trees were planted along the streets, and a machine shop, hotel, school, churches, and a department store were provided.

Post tried various forms of automatic machinery to be used in dry-land farming. In addition, he introduced different varieties of grain sorghums to the farmers. Because of unpredictable rain patterns in the area, Post initiated some spectacular rainmaking experiments, using dynamite explosions. From firing stations located along the rim of the Caprock, four-pound dynamite charges were detonated every four minutes for a period of several hours. Between 1911 and 1914, he spent thousands of dollars in these unsuccessful experiments.

Post's crop experiments showed that cotton would be the best crop for the area, so he opened a cotton mill in Post City in 1913. Thus, farmers could bring their cotton direct from field to mill. Other ideas from Post's fertile mind included feeding cattle in confinement. Today, the Texas Panhandle is the nation's largest cattle feeding area.

Post died unexpectedly after having appendicitis surgery in Santa Barbara, California. Despite his creativity and philanthropy, Post's gravestone simply gives his name, date of birth, and date of death. He was buried in Battle Creek, Michigan.

> [Post] got interested in dietetics. He was convinced that his illness and many others were rooted in people's diets ... [and] was determined to find a health food for the masses.

Captain Randolph B. Marcy

The Prairie Traveler's Companion

AN OBSCURE ARMY OFFICER, obsessed with the exploration of the great Southwest, is responsible for the naming of Big Spring, Texas, a remarkable city on the edge of the Texas High Plains.

Captain Randolph B. Marcy and other army officers were assigned the duty to scout out all the more favorable trails from Fort Smith, Arkansas, to the California gold fields in the late 1840s. Ironically, Marcy found Big Spring on his return trip from California by way of Santa Fe, New Mexico, in the fall of 1849.

A journal kept by Marcy shows that the first recorded visit by white men to what is now Big Spring and Howard County came in 1849. He had been ordered to escort and protect immigrants traveling to new territories and while doing so, find and map the best route from Arkansas to New Mexico and the west coast.

Marcy, a veteran of the U.S.–Mexican War of 1845, was a demanding officer. The captain not only mapped out the best route to California, but he also later published a book titled *The Prairie Traveler*, the classic handbook for America's pioneers.

The observant Marcy told readers of his book how to organize a company for traveling the western trails, how to select leaders, the best types of wagons and teams to use, relative merits of mules and oxen, stores and provisions, things that should be packed, amount of supplies needed, clothing, camp equipment, and firearms. He also gave recipes for the preparation of pemmican, a dried lean meat pounded into a paste with fat and preserved in the form of pressed cakes, and noted what kinds of substitutes could be used for certain kinds of foods and vegetables. Other tips in Marcy's book included facts about the weather and the availability of water.

Big Spring became important on Marcy's maps because of its supply of good water.

According to Marcy's journal or report dated November 20, 1849, he and his column of soldiers approached the Howard County-Big Spring area from the west. He wrote that he had left the Salt

Lake the morning of October 3 and headed north by east for eight miles where the group reached the border of the High Plains.

"We decended an easy slope of about 50 feet to a bench below; here we could see two bluffs in the direction that we were marching, near where our guide informed us that we could find a fine spring of water. Fourteen and a half miles of travel brought us to the spring, which was found flowing from a deep chasm in the limestone rocks into an immense reservoir of some fifty feet in depth," Marcy wrote.

Above: *Captain Randolph B. Marcy discovered Big Spring. Photo courtesy Big Spring Heritage Museum.*

Marcy's discovery of the big spring marked its existence for the immigrants moving west. The big spring quickly became a major campsite on the Overland Trail and the Santa Fe Trail. Because of the water supply, a tent city developed that helped serve travelers, trail drivers, and buffalo hunters.

The growth of western Texas can be attributed to water supplies since the first explorer traveled the broad plain in the 1600s.

Above: *The "Big Spring" that helped pioneers cross the plains. Photo courtesy* San Angelo Standard-Times.

"Early Americans had strong superstitions about springs. Heroes and gods were born out of the springs. Every Indian pueblo has sacred springs somewhere nearby. There were reasons to sanctify them—physical, as life depended on water; spiritual, for how could it be that when water fell as rain or snow and ran away or dried up there should be other water which came secretly and sweetly out of the ground and never failed," wrote Gunnar Brune, author of *Springs of Texas*, Volume I.

Indians knew how to find water. Like the coyotes before them, Indians would dig wells if their springs failed.

When the first of a series of forts were built across Texas, they were located near water resources. The forts that failed did so because of lack of potable water.

However, military leaders like Randolph B. Marcy knew that whoever controlled the water holes would control the territory.

Big Spring remained a tent city until the Texas and Pacific Railroad arrived in 1881. As a result, railroading remained Big Spring's principle industry until the 1930s when oil was discovered nearby.

Today, the "big spring" that watered wild animals, Indians, soldiers, immigrants, and even the ever-demanding boilers of the steam-powered T&P locomotives is surrounded by a beautiful park. Although the spring has not flowed an adequate supply of water in decades, its importance to the community as a historical place is assured, thanks to Captain Randolph B. Marcy, the "prairie traveler's companion."

Ben Sublett's Secret Gold Mine

Little of the precious stuff has been found in western Texas

THERE HAVE ALWAYS BEEN questions about gold and its availability in western Texas, but little of the precious stuff has ever been found. There have been plenty of rich strikes for silver, mercury, and particularly oil and gas, but there are few records of any significant gold discoveries.

Llano County, in the Texas Hill Country, owes much to its mineral resources. At one time serious mining operations were started in the county by various people, but most ended in failure. Perhaps the most extensive mining operation for precious metals was started by a Colonel Schryver of San Antonio. He started sinking a shaft on the Heath place a few miles northeast of the town of Llano. Assays of ores from that source showed good value; some small pockets there were found to contain free gold.

With the news that the Heath mine was producing ore, others made attempts to find the precious metal in the same locality. Llano citizens were interested, so much so that they would drive out from town in buggies or hacks to check on developments since the mine was in sight of the public road. The mine played out later, however, and no one ever made an attempt to reopen it.

Meanwhile, other valuable minerals were being found in the county. Perhaps the richest appearing site was at Sharp Mountain, about six miles southeast of town. C. C. Wilson and E. J. Mackey had bought the property and felt so sure of finding a gold strike they hired a work force to help open a shaft twenty-two feet deep. Veins of gold showed some value, and another shaft was opened. However, geologists soon reported that the gold was of volcanic origin, and that veins of gold and silver had come up from a depth of several thousand feet.

Perhaps the richest mineral found in Llano County was yttrium. In 1887 an ounce of pure yttrium brought $144. It was a white, chalky-looking mineral and was very expensive to separate. It was used for a filament in the electric light bulb. When a cheaper substitute was found for the lamps, it was no longer mined.

Yet the elusive miner Ben Sublett keeps popping back into the picture as the man who found a rich gold mine west of the Pecos River. Folks today still seek out the Sublett treasure, believed to be hidden in the Guadalupe Mountains.

There have been a lot of stories written about the old miner. Writer-historian J. Frank Dobie made Sublett famous in his book *Coronado's Children*. Some believe Sublett's discovery of gold is true. Was Dobie's account truthful, or was the truth stretched somewhat?

According to Dobie, Sublett came west from Missouri to prospect in the Rockies but never found enough gold to get excited about or enough to pay his expenses. While away on a prospecting trip, Sublett's wife and small children would be left for days and sometimes weeks, often going hungry while "Ol' Ben" was out chasing his dream of becoming rich.

After his wife died, Sublett tried to keep his children together. He took odd jobs with the railroad to supply the youngsters with a place to live and food for their bellies. He never lost the lure for gold, however, and continued to make trips into the mountains searching for a rich vein.

When Sublett told his drinking pals that an Apache had told him of gold being found in the Guadalupes, many thought the old man was "a little off his rocker." However, after one of his prospecting trips into the mountains, he returned to Odessa with a pouch of gold nuggets worth enough to buy whiskey for the boys for months. Ol' Ben let it be known that he had found his rich gold mine.

After this incident in Odessa, Sublett would leave out every few months for the mountains—alone. He would return a few weeks later with more sacks of gold nuggets. Many people tried to follow him, but they would lose his trail in the sands near what is now Monahans.

According to some historians, a man named Joe Flanagan was hired by a Midland banker to follow the old prospector. Lee Driver, who operated a livery stable in Midland, was said to keep a horse saddled and ready around the clock for Flanagan's use. One day Flanagan followed Sublett when he left Odessa in a buggy pulled by two burros. The trail generally followed the Texas and Pacific Railroad tracks to Pecos, then cut north up the Pecos for about twenty-five miles where the trail simply vanished. Other people reported having similar experiences while trying to follow the old miner.

After losing Sublett's trail, Flanagan came upon some travelers who said they had seen Sublett headed for Odessa in the buggy. He had a big bag of gold, and he had been gone only four days. As a result of this report, folks believed that Sublett's elusive mine was somewhere along the Pecos.

After spending too much time sipping whiskey with a friend, Mike Wilson, the old miner revealed to Wilson the location of his mine. Wilson is said to have found the mine and returned with several bags of gold but immediately went on an extended drinking binge. When he sobered up, Wilson attempted to find the mine again, but he had forgotten the way. He searched for it until he died.

Sublett also revealed the location of the mine to a carpenter named Stewart, and he agreed to take Stewart along with him on his next trip to the mine. It is assumed that Stewart was to do some carpentry work at the mine site. However, Stewart had his young son with him so he could not make the trip into the mountains. He did get a peek at the mine through a long telescope.

On his way back, Sublett stopped at Stewart's camp and showed him a large tobacco sack of nuggets. He left Stewart's camp the next morning. The next thing Stewart heard was Sublett had become ill and died unexpectedly. The old miner was buried in Odessa in 1892.

The story of Sublett's mine has never been documented. Some events are true; others are yarns that have been told and retold for generations. However, the old man always had gold to spend in his late years.

There has been some evidence that Sublett never found an actual mine. His gold cache is believed to have been a large shipment of gold nuggets that had been taken during a stagecoach robbery by

Mexican bandits and hidden in a remote canyon of the Guadalupe Mountains. Sublett's map to the gold, reportedly given to Wilson, has never been found although alleged maps have been sold to the unsuspecting public. When gold fever strikes, man will do most anything to find the riches. The Sublett mine, along with the Lost Dutchman Mine in Arizona, remains a mystery to this day.

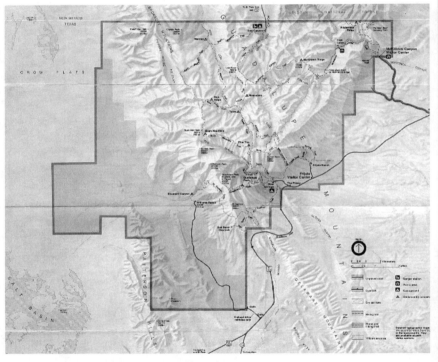

Map of Guadalupe Mountains National Park.

America's First Emperor

PROBABLY THE ONLY SIGNATURE of the United States' first and only emperor can be found at Fredericksburg, nestled in the worn, yellowed pages of a hotel register.

The signature is authentic. It actually appears twice in the register, but several years separate the two visits. What does the inscription say?

"Ulysses S. Grant, Emperor I, Washington, D.C."

The date of the entry in the old Nimitz Hotel register was Christmas Eve, 1876. U. S. Grant was then president of the United States. His later visit, on April

Right: *U. S. Grant, America's first emperor.* Photo *courtesy* San Angelo Standard-Times.

13, 1884, was just fourteen months before he died in New York in July 1885.

The Nimitz Hotel register is now safely behind glass in the Nimitz Museum of the Pacific War. However, when the hotel was still used as a lodging place in 1961, I had the opportunity to stay there and had the privilege of looking through the register. It was an eye-opening experience.

According to a story related by the late Charles B. Nimitz, the founder of the hotel, Grant is said to have arrived with three aides that Christmas Eve "well fortified" with pre-Christmas spirits. While there is no way to verify the late hotelkeeper's observation about his famous guest, the country's eighteenth president never turned down the chance to "sip some bourbon and branch water."

The Nimitz, one of the oldest hotels in the state, has a proud history and has had a number of famous people as guests. Now it is one of the state's top tourist attractions, telling the story about the Nimitz family and also providing a massive amount of information about the campaigns fought in the Pacific during World War II. The late Fleet Admiral

Chester Nimitz, a native of Fredericksburg and grandson of the hotel founder, was Commander in Chief of all Pacific Naval Forces.

Along with Grant's signature in the register, there appear the names of other famous folks from the pioneer days, including the name of C. B. Metcalfe, a pioneer rancher from Tom Green County, who then lived at Ben Ficklin. He

> The Nimitz, one of the oldest hotels in the state, has a proud history and has had a number of famous people as guests. Now it is one of the state's top tourist attractions, telling the story about the Nimitz family and also providing a massive amount of information

stayed at the hotel on May 26, 1877. Another impressive entry in the register is the signature of President Rutherford B. Hayes "with staff," who stopped there while en route to Mexico.

Along with these signatures can be found the scrawled signature of W. J. Gentry, a famous Texas gunfighter of the 1870s; Charles Harcourt, alias "Buckskin

Charlie," an early-day Indian fighter and army scout; General Phillip Sheridan, famous Civil War leader and later commander of the army; Daniel Webster, one of the country's foremost statesmen; and a man who signed the register as C. H. Howard of El Paso, alias Jesse James.

The museum also has in its collection an early-day ledger that the hotel kept. An 1853 entry is about the campaigns fought in the Pacific during World War II. The late Fleet Admiral Chester Nimitz, a native of Fredericksburg and grandson of the hotel founder, was Commander in Chief of all Pacific Naval Forces.

that of a Major James Longstreet of Fort Mason, Texas. Longstreet would later become famous as a Confederate general and confidant of General Robert E. Lee. Lee, then a colonel in the U.S. Army, also served at Fort Mason and was a hotel guest as well.

According to the ledger, among Longstreet's purchases were three pounds of coffee for 50 cents; a pair of shoes for $1; one "seegar," 5 cents; a blanket, $4.50; a quart of whiskey, 20 cents; and 32 pounds of sweet potatoes, 96 cents. It also noted that Longstreet was rather late in paying his bill.

Southwestern Texas has had lots of famous visitors over the years, but none any more famous than those who rested their road-weary bodies in Fredericksburg's Nimitz Hotel.

Today the Nimitz is best known as a historical center and museum celebrating the history of America's most famous naval battles. The place is unique because these artifacts are housed hundreds of miles from the nearest span of saltwater and a half continent away from the ocean on which these battles were fought.

Not only have I had the opportunity to stay in the old hotel while it was still a lodging place, I also had the opportunity to watch from the sidelines over the years as the National Museum of the Pacific War and the George Bush Gallery slowly developed into a truly outstanding memorial to the thousands of sailors, soldiers, marines, Seabees, coast watchers, and civilians who were caught up in the fight with Japan during World War II.

The historical center, still in various stages of development for the future, is the only complex in the world dedicated solely to telling the story of the Pacific War. And the center does a fine job of telling the story, using various kinds of media, including rare artifacts, photographs, models, and displays featuring life-size manikins and tools of war like artillery pieces, tanks, landing craft, bombers, salvaged aircraft, a Japanese midget submarine captured at Pearl Harbor, and pieces of uniforms donated by the wearers.

The Admiral Nimitz complex was started in the 1960s when Fredericksburg citizens decided to establish a memorial to honor Fleet Admiral Chester Nimitz, who was born and reared in this Hill Country town. Focal point was the old Nimitz Hotel building, which had been built by the admiral's grandfather in 1852. The structure had the appearance of a steamboat since the builder had been a riverboat captain. After years of struggle and help from various private sources and the Admiral Nimitz Foundation, funds were raised to restore the hotel to its original appearance.

In 1991, when the complex was able to acquire an adjoining piece of property that had housed a huge supermarket, work got underway to create the George Bush Gallery and the National Museum of the Pacific War. By 1995 the facade of the gallery building was completed, along with the Plaza of the Presidents, which honors the American presidents who served in America's armed forces during World War II. The facility was officially opened in June 1999 by former president George Bush, accompanied by members of his family, including President George W. Bush, who was then serving as governor of Texas.

Three main exhibit areas are in the new facility. The displays are truly spellbinding and give the visitor the feeling of "being there" and involved in the action. In one display the miniature Japanese submarine is mounted on its mother sub, plowing through the waves off the coast of Honolulu. While standing on the submarine's deck and watching the lights from Pearl Harbor and Honolulu blinking on the distant horizon, my stomach moved around some and I had a sickly feeling. I am not a good sailor, so the realistic ocean view painted by the artist Richard W. DeRosset gave me reason to move on.

The next display also was related to naval warfare with the launching of Colonel Jimmy Doolittle's B-25 bomber raid on Tokyo from the deck of the American aircraft carrier *Hornet*. The bomber on display, ready to take off from the pitching ship, is one of the few such aircraft still in good enough repair for display. It was loaned to the museum by the U.S. Air Force. It had previously been on display at Reese Air Force Base in Lubbock.

The last major exhibit in the building focuses on Henderson Field on Guadacanal Island. The battered and stripped down FM2 Wildcat Navy fighter plane is being worked on by marines. The old airplane, which was involved in a training accident a half century ago, was raised from the bottom of Lake Michigan.

The enormity of the Pacific War campaign does not allow for a complete presentation about the conflict, thus plans are being made to add another building to the complex. The new building will house other exhibits and a diorama depicting the Battle of Buna, complete with an amphibious landing. Also, visitors will be able to walk on the bridge of a cruiser and see a combat information center in operation during the Battle of Leyte Gulf. Another display will be a torpedo bomber like the one that former President Bush was piloting when he was shot down near Iwo Jima in the South Pacific in 1944. He was rescued by a submarine crew.

Please take time to visit the museum and old hotel. It is well worth your time and the cost. It is open daily 8 A.M. to 5 P.M. except on Christmas.

"Fighting Parson" Potter

And His Circuit Ridin' Brethren

ANDREW JACKSON POTTER took a long time to find the Lord, but when he did the "fighting parson" became a strong advocate of religion. The fiery preacher, best known for putting a Colt's pistol on his pulpit beside the Bible and keeping a Winchester rifle propped against the whiskey barrel or Arbuckle's Coffee box being used as a pulpit, was one of a few brave men to ride the frontier circuit. Others were the legendary Reverend William B. Bloys, who established the Bloys camp meeting near Fort Davis, and Leander Random Millican, a former East Texas cowboy who helped bring religion to the Big Bend country and who helped bring the Paisano Baptist Encampment to fruition.

These disciples of the Lord came from different backgrounds and represented different church denominations—Potter was a Methodist, Bloys was a Presbyterian, and Millican was a Baptist—but each had something in common: bringing religion to folks who did not see a church house or preacher for sometimes a year or more.

Texas in the 1870s was perhaps the most lawless place on earth. A combination of factors made it so; West Texas was frontier country, and the Comanches, Apaches, Kiowas, and others were raiding ruthlessly. In addition, the Civil War had caused much upheaval in families and unsettled the lives of normally quiet, hardworking men, and Reconstruction was causing all kinds of bitterness among the citizenry. Also, outlaws from all over the South and the border states were pouring into the state because there were few law officers to keep the peace.

No name was more familiarly known in western Texas than that of Andrew Jackson Potter. His name was a household word, ranging from the Panhandle to the Gulf of Mexico and from the Colorado to the Rio Grande. In 1872, while the U.S. Congress was considering how to protect the frontier, a member of the Texas delegation declared:

"Remove your regulars and the garrison on the Texas border: commission Jack Potter, a reclaimed desperado and now a Methodist preacher and Indian fighter; instruct him to choose and organize 100 men and the Indian depredations along the Texas border will cease."

Andy Potter was the third son of Joshua Potter, a rugged Kentucky sharpshooter who had fought the British at New Orleans. His father so admired his general and leader, "Old Hickory," that he named the son after Andrew Jackson. Andy was born in Missouri in 1830. His family, including three other boys and three girls, moved about a great deal. Times were harsh. He was an orphan at the age of ten. In order to survive, he became a jockey, and in a short time he was making his employer

Right: *Andrew Jackson Potter, the "fightin' parson."* Photo courtesy *West Texas Collection, Angelo State University.*

rich. In return, his boss taught him how to write, play cards, and shoot straight. He followed the racetracks as a rider for six years. His friends then were other jockeys, gamblers, drunkards, and others of ill repute.

When hostilities broke out between the U.S. and Mexico in 1846, the sixteen-year-old Andy Potter joined a group of volunteers where he worked as a teamster and learned to drive oxen. His first taste of Indian fighting occurred when the wagon train he was with was overwhelmed by Indians while en route to Bent's Fort on the Arkansas River.

After six years as a soldier, Potter came to Texas to visit a brother on York's Creek in Hays County. While visiting his brother, he was stricken with typhoid fever and nearly died. While living on York's Creek and working day jobs to pay off his debts, Potter heard the gospel preached by a Methodist minister, I. G. John. The text, "Who is the Wise Man?" seemed to pierce Potter's soul. Soon he was a regular in church services, even foregoing the Sunday horse races. At a great revival at Croft's Creek in 1856, Potter was converted, joined the church, and

Above: *Parson Potter with converts. Photo courtesy West Texas Collection, Angelo State University.*

gave up his horse race gambling. He became an avid Bible reader and under Rev. John's direction, soon was learning to write and to preach. He began his preaching career as a circuit rider in 1859 when he relocated to Lockhart, where he bought a small farm and got his license to preach. From there, he started his career as an itinerant preacher.

Potter was known as a reformer

but not a fanatic. He preached in saloons and gambling houses, and when the Civil War started, he joined the 32nd Texas Cavalry at Prairie Lea. He served in the ranks but was appointed chaplain of DeBray's Regiment. He participated in several battles during the Red River Campaign.

When the war concluded, Potter was appointed a supply preacher to the Prairie Lea circuit and was later stationed at Kerrville. He also was assigned to the Uvalde circuit, which carried him to the Rio Grande and the Texas-Mexico border. During this time he had a brief fight with four Indians on the road between Frio and Sabinal Canyon. Traveling in a small wagon pulled by two small Spanish mules, Potter had a time staying out of view of the Indians. When the four warriors rushed him, he wounded one and scared off the other three. His first shot was true, but the others were misfires. His ammunition was

While living on York's Creek and working day jobs to pay off his debts, Potter heard the gospel preached by a Methodist minister, I. G. John. The text, "Who is the Wise Man?" seemed to pierce Potter's soul. Soon he was a regular in church services, even foregoing the Sunday horse races.

defective. After hiding in a thicket, checking his ammunition, and cleaning his pistol and Winchester, Potter was able to escape after wounding a second Indian.

In 1878 Potter started his labors at Fort Concho. The present city of San Angelo was then a small village across the Concho River from the fort filled with saloons, gambling halls, whorehouses, and other unsavory places where soldiers could lose all their money and their lives at the drop of an insult. It was here that Potter got his reputation of having a pistol on the pulpit while preaching to the soldiers, gamblers, and plainsmen. He moved his family to San Angelo in 1883 and rode the circuit wherever he was assigned.

The fiery Potter's preaching career ended where it started. In 1894 he was assigned to preach in the Lockhart area. On October 21, 1895, while preaching at Tilden, near Lockhart, and while delivering his message with uplifted

31

hands and the words, "I believe," he fell dead at the pulpit. He was buried in the nearby Walnut Creek Cemetery. It was said of him that he knew every road, trail, and landmark through all of West Texas and was made welcome at every place he stopped.

Leander R. Millican brought his religion to the frontier about the same time as the pistol-toting Parson Potter. However, the men were different in a number of ways.

Millican was a cowboy, but he never drove cattle northward. Born August 27, 1853, where the small community of Millican is now situated in Brazos County, Millican's family was among the first 300 Austin colonists. The family settled at the big bend of the Brazos River in 1824.

At the tender age of eight, Millican was called on to carry important documents and business papers by horseback from his home to Boonville, a distance of some sixteen miles. The young horseman experienced high water on the Brazos and other streams in the area during the period. His brothers were away in the Confederate army; his father was dead. His religious awakening came during this time when the youth assumed enormous responsibility for himself and for others as well.

By the time Millican had reached his sixteenth birthday, he was carrying the mail between Lampasas and Austin, astride a little Spanish mule. Indians were then numerous in the area, so he had to keep his eyes peeled for trouble. He was chased only once but escaped when his little mule reached the post office in a "race for your whiskers," he recalled.

He started making the cow camps after completing the mail contract and hired on with rancher John Sparks in 1870. When he left the Sparks ranch in 1871, Millican was on the verge of becoming a deputy sheriff in Lampasas County, but he worked as a process server for the justice of the peace for several years. As a deputy sheriff in Lampasas later, Millican learned how to handle men who tended to get "hot under the collar" and those who tended to settle quarrels with a six-shooter. He would come into contact with some of the territory's toughest gunslingers during that time, including Lou Saw-yers and the Horrell brothers.

According to Millican's associates in later years, he seemed to always be completely at ease with rough and tough men, and the worst of the lot always seemed to know that Millican was without fear in dealing with them. One time while riding a train, he encountered a drunk who fired his six-shooter and terrified the passengers. Millican asked the conductor to do something about the troublemaker, but he refused. Millican seized the man and threw him down and told the man in a quiet, soft voice to behave. The drunk sat quietly the remainder of the trip.

Millican came face to face with his own destiny at a Methodist camp meeting on Cherokee Creek in San Saba County in the summer of 1874. Admittedly indifferent to religion until then, Millican was converted and soon had a deep desire to preach. The First Baptist Church in Lampasas had been organized the previous year, and on December 20, 1874, "after a close, prayerful study of the New Testament," Millican became a Baptist. He was baptized the following day in a cold river stream.

Shortly thereafter Millican entered Baylor University at Independence. He paid $12.50 per month for board and room. Until he entered Baylor, then a one-building institution, his main interest was ranching, freighting, and keeping law and order. Education was not high on his priority list. Millican did not complete his schoolwork at Baylor, choosing to return to the prairies and woods.

He said he got his "feet wet" in religion during the period of 1875 and 1878, when he wandered and preached as often as possible to anyone who would listen. He was ordained February 4, 1878, at the Lampasas Baptist Church and was commissioned a missionary for the San Saba Association on September 1, 1879. His salary was $35 a month. No matter how careful he was with his salary, it never covered all his expenses as he traveled his vast territory for the next fifty years!

In 1881 Millican got his first taste of western Texas. He and another missionary preacher from back east traveled to Abilene from

Lampasas to launch a mission church. During the trip by horse and buggy, the men were overtaken by a fierce blue norther with sleet, snow, and occasional rain. The seasoned Millican, toughened by other storms while working as a circuit minister, piled lap blankets and buffalo robes over his chilled companion and remained awake through the night to keep the campfire burning so they would not freeze to death. Soon after their arrival in Abilene, the men established the First Baptist Church there.

In a report presented to the Texas Baptist Association in 1884, a pattern of his life's work would clearly emerge:

"Reverend Millican has labored half his time at Burnet for 52 weeks, preached 100 sermons, received 20 new members by letter, and made 267 religious visits. The house there [church] is completed and is able to support a pastor for half his time."

Many years later Millican would recall that during early years of his ministry he traveled "always on horseback," sometimes breaking in a bronc for use in his travels. In 1888 Millican had gone to the Sweetwater Baptist Association, which covered the vast region of western Texas, stretching from Abilene to El Paso. Later he worked for the El Paso Association.

During that wild time on the Texas frontier, few churches existed, and those of record were only part time. Congregations were small and leaderless. It must have made folks feel real good to see the cowboy preacher riding up to the churchyard.

"Brother Millican is coming! Brother Millican is coming!" recalled Mrs. Barney Hubbs of Pecos when the horseback preacher would come riding up to her parents' ranch.

She told interviewers many years ago that when Pastor Millican came calling, a chicken was killed and women at the ranch immediately prepared a feast for their friend. He also was invited to spend the night, although the family was Presbyterian. Millican, as well as other circuit-riding preachers, would speak at the Union church at Toyah.

The soft-spoken Millican, called the missionary to the mountains, the circuit rider of the plains, and the sky pilot of the cowboys, eventually put his horses out to pasture and traveled by newfangled automobiles and on the train. He was still preaching when he reached his eightieth year.

Perhaps Millican's greatest achievement was helping to establish the Paisano Baptist Encampment between Alpine and Marfa. The year was 1913 when Millican, J. C. Bird, and S. C. Holmes were named to a committee to study the possibility of establishing a camp meeting in the vicinity of Alpine. The encampment continues to this day, annually drawing thousands of people to the weeklong session held in late summer.

On April 19, 1938, Millican died. When his funeral service and burial was held at Paisano Encampment, some of West Texas's leading cattlemen were his pallbearers. Dr. George Truett of Dallas, president of the Baptist World Alliance, preached the funeral sermon, and Dr. J. B. Tidwell, president of the Texas Baptist General Convention, was one of the speakers. It was a heavyweight funeral for the cowboy preacher.

Another early church leader and circuit-riding preacher was William Benjamin Bloys, a native of Tennessee whose work as a Presbyterian home missionary in western Texas resulted in the creation of Bloys Camp Meeting held annually at Skillman's Grove, near Fort Davis.

While still a youngster, W. B. Bloys moved with his family to Missouri and later to Illinois where he attended college and worked on the family farm. He was licensed to preach in May 1878 and served a number of small churches with once-a-month services.

He was later ordained by the Presbytery of Cairo, Illinois, on June 4, 1879. He hoped to serve as a missionary in India, but he was unable to pass the physical examination for overseas work. Thus, he entered the home missionary field at the urging of his friend, Dr. Henry Little, who was superintendent of home missions for Texas. Bloys' first assignment was in Coleman, where he delivered his first sermon in a two-story building. When the sound of clinking glasses reached his ears, he soon realized that the ground floor was being used as a saloon. Bloys utilized the building as his church until a suitable building was constructed several years later. He and his wife, Isabelle, started their family in Coleman. In 1885 the town started a community library at the urging of the couple. The library remains active to this day.

Bloys' later assignment to the western area of Texas came as a result of a serious illness he had in the winter of 1886-87 when he came down with measles while attending a meeting at Runnels, once a thriving community in the adjoining county. Traveling by horseback in the severe cold, Bloys was seriously ill when he reached home. When his health continued to be of concern, he was advised by his doctors to move to a higher, drier climate.

A Coleman family, the David Merrills, had started ranching near Fort Davis. They invited Bloys and his family to come to the mountains and asked the preacher to help revitalize the Fort Davis church congregation. They arrived in Fort Davis on February 22, 1888, in a snowstorm.

The Presbyterian church assigned the Reverend Bloys all the territory west of the Pecos River, so he started on horseback to visit everyone in his mission field, no matter how isolated the ranches were or how small the groups. During these lengthy journeys, he baptized children into whatever faith the parents wished, performed marriages, conducted funerals, and helped with the injured and the ill. Often he would change into overalls and help with the ranch chores. Being a preacher on the frontier was not an easy life.

After serving the Fort Davis community and surrounding area for several years, Bloys was approached by the John Z. Means family, who lived west of the mountains, about starting a camp meeting so that isolated ranch families could benefit from religious worship and fellowship. Many of the early settlers in the Davis Mountains had Deep South roots where the first camp meetings were held in the late 1700s, thus these folks brought the camp meeting tradition with them as they traveled westward.

The first camp meeting was organized on October 10, 1890. Cowboys and others carried the news about the camp meeting, which was to be held at Skillman's Grove, a historic site on the westward trail. Forty-seven people attended that first camp meeting, bringing with them wagons loaded with camping supplies and other equipment. The first meeting lasted two days, and Reverend Bloys preached three sermons each day. A huge oak tree, located in the grove, provided shelter for those attending services. It was later named the "Union Tree."

From its meager beginnings, Bloys Camp Meeting became one of the most important events in West Texas, drawing thousands of people to the picturesque site along the old San Antonio-El Paso Road.

"Every denomination will be welcome here," proclaimed Bloys "There will be no lines drawn because of different religious beliefs. Everyone is welcome to come and worship with us."

As the years passed, the camp meeting grew into somewhat of a social event as well. Many ranch women, who often went for months without seeing another woman, had an opportunity to share experiences with each other, thus the social aspect became nearly as important as the religious one.

During the first eleven years, services were conducted under a brush arbor. A new one was constructed each year. However, the camp meeting was growing at such a rate that plans were made to put up a permanent meeting hall. Today, a pavilion provides space for services, and many early families have set up separate camps where they sleep and eat.

Potter, Millican, Bloys, and the many other circuit-riding preachers of frontier times could be described today as pioneer shepherds, bringing their "flocks" together. Through their hard work, determination, and dedication to God, religion came to the wild and woolly West.

William Leslie Black

WEALTHY COTTON BROKER, successful West Texas rancher, inventor, soldier, sailor, convicted pirate. Colonel William L. Black of Fort McKavett in Menard County was all of these things and more. He was perhaps Texas's most successful frontier entrepreneur.

Born in New Orleans on August 3, 1843, Black was of Scottish-English ancestry. He was one of four sons of a successful middle-class businessman, Charles Black of Elgin, Scotland, who operated a mercantile firm specializing in overseas cotton trade.

Black's mother, Agnes Sewell, was born in Liverpool, England, in 1819. She and Charles Black married in New Orleans in 1837, and the couple had ten children, including Alexander Gordon, John Fisher, William Leslie, Charles Edmond, Eleanor, and another daughter who later married George Vennard. Four other children died in infancy.

The Civil War destroyed New Orleans cotton merchant Black financially, and he never reentered the cotton business after the war, choosing to reside in Kirkwood, Missouri, until his death in 1884 at the age of sixty-seven.

At the age of nineteen, William Leslie Black and his brother Charles Edmond enrolled in the Confederate army in 1862, volunteering to serve the customary ninety days in a volunteer Louisiana regiment called the "Crescent." Within a short period of time, the Black brothers were assigned duty in Mississippi under the command of General Pierre T. Beauregard. Two days after joining Beauregard's regiment, both young men were seriously wounded at the Battle of Shiloh.

After recovering from his wounds, Black promised his mother not to reenlist in the army. However, he went to the Bahamas to work with his brother Alexander Gordon, who was shipping cotton to England by running the Union blockade off the southern coast.

While in the Bahamas, Black met Lieutenant Thomas Hogg, a Confederate navy officer. Hogg had been commissioned to form an expedition to capture the steamer *Guatemala* or its sister ship *San Salvador*, both of which

Right: *Colonel William Black, frontier entrepreneur. Photo courtesy West Texas Collection, ASU.*

made semimonthly trips between Panama and Guatemala. Once pirated, the captured vessel would be used to destroy the Pacific whaling fleet and terrorize U.S. commerce, sending the captured spoils to the beleaguered Confederacy.

Bleck kept his promise to his mother about not joining the army. He didn't say anything about not joining the navy, so he signed up with Hogg's raiders.

Unfortunately for Black, his friend Hogg, and their companions, the raiders were caught by Union troops while on board the *San Salvador*. The whole bunch was taken to San Francisco where they were jailed at Fort Alcatraz, which was later to become an infamous federal prison for America's most hardened criminals.

After a lengthy trial, the "San Salvador pirates" were convicted of espionage and sentenced to death by hanging on the gallows at San Quentin prison.

A model prisoner during his incarceration, Black became the prison's bookkeeper. With the support of the warden, help from wealthy San Francisco banker D. J. Tallent, and support of influential friends in Washington, Black was pardoned in December 1865.

Although he could have returned to Louisiana, Black remained in California to help get his shipmates released. He finally accomplished this in May 1866 then returned to the Gulf Coast port city to begin civilian life.

Black considered many ventures, including starting a fishing fleet and investing in copper mines, but ended up in the wholesale fruit and nut business. When this business venture failed, he returned to the cotton trade and went to New York.

Cotton trading was a tradition in the Black family, and all the sons became interested in the trade after the war. But William Leslie's interest in cotton started early in life when he left school to work for his father's merchandising firm. Here, working alongside his father, William Leslie was able to gain experience in the overseas cotton trade, a business that he would one day make his own.

Records of William Leslie Black's life and activities in New York are rather sketchy, although it is clear that he immersed himself in his business.

When Black entered the cotton trade in New York, there was no organized trading system of the fiber, thus he and some older cotton merchants cooperated to establish and develop the New York Cotton Exchange. The year 1869 was a momentous one for Black. He became the 35th charter member of the Exchange's 100 charter members. He later was to acquire a farm in Virginia where he planted an orchard of orange trees and developed an oyster bed in preparation for another enterprise.

Perhaps the most important event was his marriage to Camilla Bogert, the pretty twenty-year-old daughter of George C. Bogert, a New Yorker who had gone to New Orleans as a young man to enter the shipping business. His daughter, Camilla, was born there in 1849.

Although successful and wealthy, Black was not satisfied with his Virginia farm, orchard, or cotton trading business, so he sought new challenges.

Having traveled extensively, Black concluded that St. Louis had potential as a future cotton market because it was rapidly becoming a railroad center. In 1873 Black sold his New York Cotton Exchange membership and moved his family to Missouri.

As Black predicted, the market for cotton in St. Louis grew rapidly. However, St. Louis cotton brokers needed better facilities to conduct business, so he and other colleagues built an impressive cotton exchange building there. He also persuaded the city of St. Louis to allow the cotton merchants to use the building rent free if the brokers promised to occupy it for fifty years. In gratitude, the other brokers gave Black a huge $65,000 bonus and an elegant eight-piece sterling silver service. The pieces have remained in the family since that time.

Always seeking new challenges, Black became interested in West Texas and in ranching when he determined that wool was a more profitable commodity than cotton. He had traveled in western Texas on several occasions, so he decided to buy a ranch. He chose a 30,000-acre parcel of land on the headsprings of the San Saba River in 1876. The land, which was located in what later became Menard and Schleicher Counties, was purchased from a man named Robert Robinson at ten cents an acre. The parcel also encompassed an abandoned army fort.

Throughout his life, Black kept a diary, although in those days he referred to it as his "copybook."

In early 1873 Black reported in his copybook his interest in the rich resources of Texas, and during one of his exploratory trips in 1876, he bought the Fort McKavett ranch. Later he reported on the purchase of the land:

"I only paid 10 cents an acre for the land, and I was thought to be an escaped lunatic from a St. Louis insane asylum for buying the land," he wrote. "The land suited me, and I thought, with the splendid spring I got with my purchase and a 300-acre pecan grove, it was reasonably cheap."

Black stocked his new ranch with 700 head of longhorn cattle, 1,000 sheep, and a carload of purebred Merino rams. In subsequent years Black's land accumulations would total 80,000 acres, and he would run 7,000 cattle and 20,000 sheep.

But in 1876 Black knew absolutely nothing about the ranching business. He hired an English remittance man named Douglas Shannon to operate the ranch while he remained in St. Louis. Unfortunately, Shannon knew no more about running a ranch than Black, but he was in charge of the place for five years.

One of the first things that Shannon did as manager was to post notices all over the ranch giving instructions and rules for operating the place. According to Edith Black Winslow's book *In Those Days*, some of Shannon's regulations included:

1. Intemperance, sleeping late, going home to dinner during the time men should be tending the cattle will be considered good reason for discharge.

2. Herders are permitted to milk for their own family use, but for no other purpose, and must look after the cows kept for their use.

3. When prairie fires occur, all hands are expected to assist in fighting fires day and night.

4. Early to work at all times. No delay for milking; penned cattle must be turned out and herders go on their rounds early every morning.

Neighbors and some of the employees, like Charlie Adams who later helped found the town of Sonora, thought Shannon an odd sort of a man. Besides posting notices all over the forty-six-section ranch, he also bathed daily in the river, even in winter when the ice was thick.

Black's ranching adventure is a story in itself. He operated the ranch by long distance—an occasional visit and lots of correspondence—until he and his family moved to Fort McKavett in 1883.

The family traveled from St. Louis to Abilene by rail, then covered the last 125 miles by wagon. The Blacks, with three women household servants and the family dogs, rode in two army ambulances, wagons containing two seats and covered with curtains that could be rolled down in bad weather. Tagging along behind were seven covered wagons loaded with household goods, supplies, and furniture.

After arriving at the abandoned army fort, the family lived in the old fort hospital building for about eighteen months until the twelve-room ranch house was completed nearly two miles away.

While Black's wife, Camilla, and the three women house servants cared for the couple's nine children, Black went about learning the ranch business, constantly seeking ways to make the ranch profitable.

Black prospered in West Texas. When he arrived he sold all his cattle at a good profit and entered the sheep business on a massive scale. When his English manager, Shannon, moved on, Black hired Tom Palmer as his cattle foreman and A. B. Priour to be sheep foreman.

In spite of making money with his sheep, Black saw problems arising in the sheep and wool industry, including a big drop in prices whereby wool dropped from twenty cents a pound in 1884 to seven cents a pound in 1885 when Black sold his first clip through Theodore Heick's new warehouse at Abilene.

Due to the wool price drop, Black restocked his ranch with cattle and kept some sheep on an additional 32,000 acres that he leased adjacent to his home ranch.

A radical move was made by Black soon after restocking with cattle. He put up the first barbed wire fence around his place at an enormous cost, but Black reasoned that it would eventually be necessary. His foresight proved correct.

Black wrote in his copybook that the low wool price was due to President Grover Cleveland trying to make the United States a free trade country.

"This convinced me that he [Cleveland] must have also been in an insane asylum at some time in his life," Black observed.

In 1889 Black was named a Texas delegate to a national meeting of wool growers in Washington, D.C. Sheep prices had dropped to seventy-five cents a head, and the group was lobbying for a tariff to protect growers from Mexican and Australian competition. Within a short time, the price of sheep improved to three dollars a head when the Congress voted a tariff on imports.

Because of his efforts, Black headed a committee of the National Wool Growers Association that worked for forty-two years to establish a wool exchange and a system of trading in wool futures. The colonel failed to see his long-term project become a reality. On May 18, 1931, only a week after his death, trading in wool futures began on Exchange boards. He had visualized this system as a way of putting the wool business in the hands of the producers.

Although Black did not live long enough to see wool futures traded, he did play an integral part in developing the Texas Angora goat industry. In an effort to offset another economic crisis threatening the ranch in the early part of 1890, Black bought 7,000 Angora goats. He saw the goats as potentially doubling their value because they could provide a cheap way to clear brush-infested land and at the same time produce mohair fiber.

But within two years Black found himself in another financial crisis. His Angora goat herd had increased to more than 8,000 head, and he had no market for them. Northern markets were strongly prejudiced against goats because of their being portrayed as trash eaters, thus he met strong resistance when he tried to sell the animals.

Black relates in his book *A New Industry* that he offered the meat packing giant Armour and Company of Chicago 1,000 fat wethers "at their own price" if the firm would return the hides. But company officials turned down Black's proposition, saying they could not sell that much goat meat. Armour advised Black to slaughter the goats for their hides and tallow and pack the meat in cans labeled "Roast Mutton."

Thus, Texas's first meat packing, canning, and rendering plant and tannery went into business along the banks of the San Saba River just about one and a half miles west of Fort McKavett.

Black sent to Chicago for an experienced canner, W. G. Tobin, who set about building a cannery on the colonel's ranch as soon as he arrived. Several sizes of cans were ordered, magnificent four-color labels were printed, and the Range Canning Company of Fort McKavett, Texas, USA, was in business.

Tobin's canning operations went smoothly, but the sales department had problems almost immediately. Texans and a lot of other potential consumers of his "Boiled Mutton" product had an ingrained prejudice against eating "mutton," whether it was boiled, baked, or roasted.

Again, the resourceful Black came up with a solution. The Range Canning Company went into the chili con carne business. New labels were ordered touting W. G. Tobin's Chili Con Carne. Black was able to contract all his product to a Chicago packer provided that the packer would take enough additional "chili con carne" to fill the balance of the two-pound cans on hand. The shipment of chili con carne was ultimately sold by the Chicago merchant to European consumers, so there is no record of its market acceptance.

The cannery and tannery were labor intensive, so Black had to build a row of small houses and a commissary for his workers. He was the area's largest employer at the time, having some eighty or more men on the payroll. The tannery prepared and specialized in colorfully dyed Angora skins and later tanned various wildlife hides as well.

Power for the tannery and cannery was supplied by a water wheel, which Black had installed after damming up the headwaters of the San Saba River. Years after the cannery, tannery, and tallow rendering plant had been closed, Black continued to get inquiries about the venture from all over the country. Little remains of the operation now, but rock and cement structures can still be seen along the riverbanks where the water wheel was installed.

Black's creative mind continued to churn out ideas that would be beneficial to his ranch operation and to others as well. He wrote and published a book on the Angora goat industry in 1900 that was for some time the only reference material available on goats and mohair. He also invented a new nonfriction rod for windmills, secured a patent on a fireproof house, which was a forerunner of the sprinkler system, and invented a pecan nut sheller.

Black also had not forgotten his days in the cotton business. While ranching, he took time to invent a cotton-picking machine, designed to offset the loss incurred when heavy rains caused the cotton bolls to close prematurely. The device opened the bolls and removed the seeds.

In 1913 Black's wife, Camilla, suffered a severe stroke, so he decided to move to Brownwood where better medical care was available. The ranch was leased and household goods were distributed among the children. The Blacks lived with their son and daughter, Robert and Edith, until Camilla died in March 1916.

Colonel Black, now in his seventies, spent his remaining years visiting his children and writing his memoirs. He continued to headquarter on his Fort McKavett ranch, now owned by his grandson, L. Leslie Jones. The colonel died of a stroke in 1931. He was eighty-eight years old.

Black left a tremendous legacy to western Texas. He could have retired to his native New Orleans, but he chose to relocate to the frontier and to Fort McKavett where his accomplishments set an example for others to follow. Western Texas and the livestock industry is indeed richer because of the choice he made more than a century ago.

Teacher's Life a Mystery

She Was Mighty Young to Be in the Schoolroom

SHE WAS MIGHTY YOUNG to be a frontier schoolmarm, but a lot of teachers in those wild and woolly days were chosen simply because they could read, write, and count well enough to show others how to do it.

There's not much accurate information available about the mysterious Minnie Scarborough, the eighteen-year-old school-teacher buried in a single plot of ground in the Camp San Saba Community Cemetery. Inscribed on her simple grave marker is this: "Fredonia School Teacher," her name, and the years of her life, 1880 to 1898.

Unfortunately, McCulloch and Mason County history books do not list a Minnie Scarborough as being a teacher at any of the early-day schools in northern Mason County or in southern McCulloch County.

Perhaps she had wanted to be a teacher but had not conducted any classes at the time of her death. She apparently was buried at Camp San Saba in 1898 because the Fredonia community did not have a burial ground at that time. The Pontotoc Ceme-tery, perhaps the closest to Fredonia, was closed in 1888 after a typhoid fever outbreak nearly wiped the town out in 1887.

Fredonia was first called Barton Springs and was not established as a Mason County community until 1886.

According to county records, the first Fredonia teacher was named Donnie Redmond. The first school was a small, one-room building of frame construction. It was soon replaced by a two-story frame building with the upper floor rented to the Woodsmen of the World fraternal organization.

Although there are no records of Minnie Scarborough drawing pay as a teacher, it was not unusual for that period of time for a young woman to teach pupils that, at times, might be older than she.

While seeking information about the Scarborough woman, I found some interesting facts about the school in the neighboring community of Katemcy, also in Mason County. The Katemcy school also was a one-story

Left: *Graves†
of Minnie
Scarborough,
frontier
schoolteacher.*
Photo courtes
San Angelo
Standard-Tin

building constructed in 1883, on land given by the Baptist preacher, Lawson Jones. A description of the building in the Mason County Historical Book revealed that the structure had double doors and plenty of windows for light. The seats were made of wide boards with slat backs. Desks were attached to the backs of the seats with a space beneath for books. There also was a place for an ink-well on top of the desk for each pupil. Each of these seats would accommodate from six to eight children. There were two rows on each side of the building with boys sitting on one side and girls seated on the other side. Each child paid a tuition fee of $1 to $1.50 per month, and those who could not afford to pay were assigned chores to do at the school each day. Chores ranged from cutting and hauling wood for the school stoves to building fires, sweeping the schoolhouse, and cleaning the schoolyard and playground. Subjects taught were basic arithmetic, geography, reading, and penmanship.

In 1887 the Katemcy schoolteacher, J. M. Heatherly, was paid $40 per month. Others teaching in the Mason rural schools during the years 1886 through 1890 got from $21 to $50 per month.

When a teacher at Pontotoc attempted to expand subjects to include physiology, the study of the body, the teacher received the following note from a student's mother:

"Please teach my girl how to read, write, add and subtract. Do not teach her about guts and bones, or bathing."

Teachers had few teaching materials in those early formative days, and subjects were expanded only when a full line of McGuffy books was available to the pupils and the teachers.

There are other teachers like Minnie Scarborough who are forgotten, but their mark on the development of western Texas will always remain strong in memory.

The Camp San Saba Cemetery is a short distance from the abandoned Camp San Saba schoolhouse just off U.S. Highway 87 about ten miles south of Brady near the San Saba River bridge.

Camp San Saba is one of the oldest communities in Central Texas, having been established as an outpost of Fort Mason before the Civil War. It served at one time as a permanent camp for early-day Texas Rangers.

"Guinea Pigs in Zoot Suits"

The Women Had to Prove They Could Be Ferry Pilots

When the United States entered World War II there was a serious shortage of pilots. Almost simultaneously, two efforts were organized to recruit women pilots to overcome this shortage and to free male pilots for combat duty.

The U.S. Army Air Force directed noted aviator Nancy Harkness Love to start a training program for women in which they would be trained to ferry aircraft for the Air Transport Command. The group, commissioned as the Women's Auxiliary Ferrying Squadron in September 1942, was stationed at the New Castle Army Air Base in Wilmington, Delaware.

A short time later another woman aviator, Jacqueline Cochran, was appointed director of the Women's Flying Training Detachment, independent of Love's WAFS, by General Henry H. "Hap" Arnold, chief of the Army Air Force. Cochran had just returned from England where she had brought twenty-five women pilots to ferry aircraft for the British Air Transport Authority at the request of the British government. This was the first organized group of American women pilots to serve in the war.

In 1940 and 1941 both Cochran and Love had proposed separately to U.S. military officials that American women be sought out, but their plans were not approved at the time because there were more male pilots than there were airplanes. Also, General Arnold had expressed doubts about whether women could fly large aircraft.

The first class of Cochran's

Above: *WASP trainee Francie Meisner Park gets a leg up on her plane at Avenger Field. Photo courtesy The Woman's Collection, Texas Woman's University.*
Left: *WASP founder Jacqueline Cockran. Photo courtesy The Woman's Collection, Texas Woman's University.*

319th WFTD, called the "guinea pigs," started their training at the Municipal Airport in Houston in November 1942, one month after the WAFS was formed. The airport did not house the women trainees. There were no facilities, and what was there was mostly primitive. Leoti Deaton, who was assigned the job of finding accommodations for the women, ended up housing them in hotels, motels, and private homes. Trucks were sent to pick the women up each morning and to take them to the airport for their various training exercises. For the first few weeks, there was no place to change clothes, and there were no uniforms for the women. Instead, they wore GI overalls, called "zoot suits" because they were so baggy and ill fitting.

Ruth Florey, a vivacious grandmother, told of her experiences in the Women's Airforce Service Pilots, as the group was later named, during a meeting of the Permian Historical Society held in Odessa.

Smartly dressed in her tailored Santiago blue uniform, then fifty years old, the former World War II flier gave personal insight into her experiences while in training and also as a ferry pilot. The occasion was the fiftieth anniversary of the WASP organization.

Mrs. Florey's presentation was of particular interest to historians because the WASP units were quickly disbanded after World War II came to an end. However, during its short span of existence, the

1,074 women pilots who won their wings flew more than 60 million miles, ferrying all kinds of fighter planes and bombers to the war zones.

Florey was among those first trainees to enter the flying program at Houston's Municipal Airport in 1942.

"It was an unpleasant experience," she said, recalling that the women had to ride a trolley from their rundown lodgings to the airport and that the closest cafe was a mile away. Sixty women had to share one bathroom.

She said that women were discriminated against by the male pilots who thought their training program was a fluke. "If you think discrimination in the Old West was bad, you ought to try and get an airplane away from a man," she said with a laugh.

When the women arrived in Houston to train, they wore what clothes they brought with them. Since no flying clothes were issued, the women wore the ill-fitting GI coveralls.

When the Houston base commander, Leoti Deaton, learned that a general was coming to inspect the trainees and the facilities, she went to work to find suitable uniforms for the women. When they lined up for the scheduled inspection in their dress tan slacks and shirts, the general failed to show up, Mrs. Florey recalled.

In early 1943 the women were moved to Avenger Field at Sweetwater. They were required to pay their own way there and the return fare if they washed out. They also had to pay for their own room and board.

Florey said that Avenger Field was a training base for British Royal Air Force cadets, but on August 1, 1942, the cadets were replaced with U.S. Army Air Force student pilots. When the WASP trainees arrived in 1943, Avenger Field became the only military co-educational flying field in U.S. history.

When the seven-month flying course for women was first started, most of the trainees had some actual flying experience, thus training included 180 hours of ground school and 118 hours of flight training. Later, as nonexperienced women entered the flying program, training was extended to 285 hours of ground school and 210 hours of flight training. Flight training was equally divided between PT-17s, BT-13s, and AT-6 aircraft.

In August 1943 the WFTDs and the WAFS were merged into one command called the Women's Airforce Service Pilots, with Cochran as director.

Although Cochran attempted to recruit women from all geographic areas of the country, she felt unable to accept black female pilots who applied, believing that their presence would perhaps put added pressure on the program's shaky stability, which was not altogether popular among some members of Congress or members of the military high command.

After completing training, the women were assigned to ferry duty, which meant the WASPs flew everything the Army had, from light observation planes to heavy bombers and speedy fighter planes. They towed targets for antiaircraft artillery gunners and flew tracking, smoke laying, searchlight, strafing, and simulated bombing missions.

"When you were assigned ferry duty, you never knew what kind of plane you would be flying," Mrs. Florey said. "Some had to learn quickly how to handle the controls because you could not back out of the trip."

Thirty-eight women were killed while serving in the WASPs. However, of the number of pilots trained, the WASPs had an outstanding safety record that was better than most male cadet classes, she said. The danger was not just flying the planes, Mrs. Florey said, recalling that while flying out of Liberty Field in Georgia, the women had to chase alligators and wild pigs off the runway before taking off.

"That field was built in a swamp," she explained.

Graduates of Avenger Field went on to assignments all over the U.S. They ferried 12,650 planes of 77 different types, including B-17s and B-24s, the backbone of the American bomber squadrons flying missions over Germany. According to government records, 50 percent of the fighter planes manufactured were ferried by WASPs.

The WASP program began on a civilian basis because it was an experiment, Mrs. Florey noted. While the women fliers functioned much like military units did, they lived under civilian law. They did not receive government insurance, and hospitalization for sickness or injury was difficult to arrange. A bill introduced in Congress in 1944 proposing that the WASP program be included in military operations was defeated, largely because of lobbying by male civilian pilots. By late 1944, with the war in Europe nearly over, there was a surplus of pilots, thus the Air Force determined there was no longer a need for the WASPs and the program was discontinued.

The program, which began as an experiment to see if women could handle the duties of military pilots, was successful. About 25,000 women applied to be WASPs, of which 1,800 were accepted for training. Of that number, 1,074 graduated.

In 1977, nearly thirty-five years after their official deactivation, the U.S. government gave the WASPs honorable discharges and provided them with veterans' benefits.

A memorial to the WASPs has been established at Avenger Field, now Sweetwater Municipal Airport. In addition to a monument, a walk of honor also has been integrated into the memorial in which the name of every woman who trained there will be included.

Avenger Field will always be remembered as the only all-female air base in history. After WASP training was discontinued in December 1944, the field's facilities were expanded to support the combat training of P-47 Thunderbolt pilots, but the end of the war in August 1945 brought about a rapid phase-out of all training there and elsewhere.

Since its closing at the end of World War II, the base has been used by the Air Force two other times. It was leased to the Air Force as an auxiliary field for training pilots who were assigned to Webb Air Force Base at Big Spring during the Korean War. Later it was made the site of an aircraft control and radar warning installation. It was finally released to the city of Sweetwater on November 30, 1969. Besides serving general aviation, the airfield is the site of the Texas State Technical Institute, which opened on July 31, 1970.

Pancho Villa, Bandit-General

Fights Movie War With Real Bullets

PEOPLE WILL DO STRANGE THINGS FOR MONEY, including fighting a movie war with real bullets. It happened in 1914, and the movie's star was Mexican bandit-general Pancho Villa.

While helping a writer friend do some research on the Mexican Revolution, I happened on to this story about Pancho Villa signing a contract with the Mutual Film Corporation of New York. Villa, desperate for funds to buy supplies, arms, and ammunition for his rag-tag Constitutionalist army, agreed to sell the film rights to the revolution he was fighting for $25,000 and a share in the profits.

According to information gathered by a man named Irvin Ross, the deal happened this way: Villa was getting a lot of front-page publicity in the nation's major newspapers and magazines. He had made friends with influential writers, including John Reed, who would later go on to become a leader in the American Communist Party. Reed was sent to Mexico in late 1913 to cover the revolution for *Metropolitan,* a widely read magazine whose writers included the leading gossip spreaders and reformers of the time. He also was named a correspondent for the *New York World.* Reed's articles from Mexico established him as one of the top journalists of the day. It was natural for him to become a spokesman for the film company as well.

Because of the publicity, Villa had become the symbol of the bloody revolt that gripped Mexico and that put fear into Americans living along the Texas-Chihuahua border. Photographs of the bandit-general leading his horsemen out of the hills of Chihuahua had made him Mexico's Man of the Hour.

During his earlier years living in El Paso, Villa had become acquainted with moving pictures. He and his aunt would attend the movies to get away from their dirt-floored hut in Juarez, just across the Rio Grande from El Paso. Villa may not have been able to read or write, but he was smart. Movies could show him and his dirt-poor soldiers winning the war in northern Mexico, and perhaps a film of his exploits and successes would attract American dollars to help buy horses, cannon, guns, and ammunition.

When a Mutual Film Corporation representative in El Paso wired movie company president Harry Aitken that Villa wanted to sell movie rights to his battles, Aitken wasted no time in putting the deal into motion.

On January 3, 1914, Mutual representative Frank Thayer crossed the Rio Grande and met with Villa in a Juarez hotel. Thayer told the general that the movie company would pay him $25,000 and a percentage of the film's profits.

"All you have to do is fight your battles in the daytime—between 9 A.M. and 4 P.M.—so they can be photographed," Thayer reportedly told Villa.

Villa agreed and signed the contract; thus began the first and only war in history coordinated with a movie-shooting schedule.

Meanwhile, various American news agencies also wanted first-hand photographs of the war. Robert Dorman, who would later become general manager of Acme News Pictures in New York City, was among a number of freelance photographers who joined the guerrilla bands roaming northern Mexico.

Dorman and his photographer partner, E. C. Aultman of El Paso, acquired and fitted out a railroad freight car with darkroom equipment. When Villa's troops boarded the trains to go fight, Dorman hitched his freight car to the train and went along. He was a companion of John Reed's in Villa's famous advance on Torreon and later was present at the fight at Gomez Palacio.

Like most of the revolutionary chieftains, Villa was partial to photographers and cameramen from Mutual Film Company and the correspondents. When Villa struck his deal with Mutual, the company also sent a special railroad car into Mexico, complete with darkroom and all necessary photographic equipment. When Villa's troop trains pulled away from the rail yards, the film company's camera car was attached. At times, several such cars containing the photographers and correspondents would go along to witness an attack or battle.

Reed's first real experience in gathering news stories about the Mexican Revolution occurred at Ojinaga. He arrived in the dusty border town of Presidio in late December 1913. Troops of the Mexican dictatorship had been beaten in Cuidad Juarez and Tierra Blanca, and all roads out of Chihuahua had been closed by revolutionaries. General Salvador Mercado had to leave the state of Chihuahua by the only way open to him—through the town of Ojinaga.

Right: Pancho Villa at the Battle of Ojinaga, Mexico. Photo courtesy West Texas Collection, ASU.

On November 12, 1913, Mercado left Chihuahua with 6,000 soldiers and several hundred terrified civilians. It took Mercado's army fifteen days to cross a desert stretching some 300 kilometers. The tract was called the "caravan of death" by some newspapers. Mercado had lost about half his troops before arriving at Ojinaga, where troops of villista chiefs Panfilo Natra and Toribio Ortega were already dug in on hills overlooking the village.

In Reed's book *Insurgent Mexico*, first published in 1914, he gives a vivid description of both Presidio, Texas, and its Mexican neighbor, Ojinaga.

"At Presidio, on the American side of the river, one could climb to
the flat mud roof of the post office and look across the mile of low
scrub growing in the sand to the shallow, yellow stream; and beyond
to the low mesa, where the town was, sticking sharply up out of the
scorched desert, ringed with bare, savage mountains."

Later, during the siege when Villa's troops bombarded Ojinaga,
Presidio residents could watch the fight across the river. Several
overhead water storage tanks in Presidio were peppered with rifle
bullets, and more than one artillery round whizzed overhead, recalled
the late Big Bend ranch woman Hallie Crawford Stillwell, who taught
school in the border town.

Reed wrote that Ojinaga's square, gray adobe houses could easily
be seen, along with the Oriental cupola of the old Spanish church.
During the day, federal soldiers in shabby white uniforms scurried
about the place, digging trenches and rifle pits, making ready for Villa
and his Constitutionalist army, which was rumored to be on its way.

The last of the major *federales* armies was holed up in Ojinaga, and
rebel General Ortega was unable to dislodge Mercado's troops from
their fortified positions.

By December 10, 1913, a battle was expected to begin at any hour.
Piles of household goods of every description were being brought
into Presidio by Ojinaga residents seeking refuge from the forthcoming fight. U.S. officials sent additional border patrolmen to Presidio to
help maintain order. Refugees and federal troops escaping from Chihuahua City could be seen for miles across the desert south of the
town. Civilian refugees waded the shallow Rio Grande as quickly as
they could.

Presidio, itself not more than a village, now had hundreds of refugees, a detachment of American army troops, curious onlookers,
movie crews, newspaper reporters, and photographers gathered to
observe the spectacle. Skirmishes between the *federales* and
revolutionaries started on December 12, 1913, and reinforcements
were sent to Presidio from Fort Bliss in El Paso on the same day by
special train to Marfa. With the addition of four troops from the 13th

Cavalry Regiment, numbering about 250 men, the American army presence at Presidio now totaled more than 500 soldiers. The extra troops were badly needed. Presidio had exploded in population in a few days' time. The town was awash with frightened and homeless people who slept on the ground and ate whatever was available.

On December 22, 1913, three brigades of rebel soldiers, numbering about 3,000 men, were reported en route from Chihuahua City to Ojinaga with Pancho Villa in command. The main attack came on a bitter cold Christmas Day, and the fighting continued for days while additional refugees crossed the river into Presidio to huddle in abject misery in cold and sleet.

Another motion picture camera crew, headed by Charles Pryor of El Paso Feature Film Company, recorded some spectacular motion pictures of the main rush of refugees crossing the Rio Grande on December 31. Pryor had three reels of film that showed vivid pictures of the suffering of both refugees and Mexican federal troops that had surrendered to the U.S. Army as they trudged on foot the sixty-five miles to Marfa, where they were taken by train to El Paso for imprisonment at Fort Bliss.

Villa then showed how vicious he could be, ordering the execution of any stragglers and suspected sympathizers of the federal cause while hamming it up for the movie cameras in the streets of Ojinaga.

When Villa attacked Ojinaga, the movie cameras were there. When Villa's artillery officers put their cannons into position to shell the federal troops that were dug in at Ojinaga, he refused to give the order to fire until the cameras were in position. The army had to wait two hours before starting one assault because Mutual's chief cameraman, L. M. Burrud, was not ready.

In another brutal action, Villa also ordered a cannon barrage on a distant hillside so that the Mutual film crew could get shots of the shells landing on the federal positions, sending bodies flying into the air. In another battle, Burrud actually took over command, not allowing assault troops to fire on federal cavalry until they were in close range.

But Villa the movie star became difficult to work with. He wanted more film exposure than that given to his armies. When the cans of film were sent to New York and put together, there was little fighting and too much Villa, strutting like a rooster. The first showing of the film was a disaster. Something had to be done.

Harry Aitken, the head of Mutual, made a trip to see Villa in March 1914 and bluntly told the general that the film was "no good." However, Mutual was willing to try again. Villa was elated and agreed to give the film company "a better war this time."

After getting footage of Villa's camp followers, the *soldados*, and the countryside, the camera crew left. The footage was turned over to legendary filmmaker D. W. Griffith, maker of the historic film *Birth of A Nation*. However, Griffith was unable to do much with the film. It was again a dud at the box office. The negative eventually disappeared, never to be seen again. Some still shots taken from the film remain in some collections around the country.

Twenty years later Pancho Villa appeared on the motion picture screen again; this time Hollywood actor Wallace Beery played the title role. Villa didn't get to see the movie. He was in his grave, having been assassinated at Parral several years earlier.

A postscript to this story is essential:
On March 9, 1916, Villa's forces swooped down upon the border town of Columbus, New Mexico. The attack was attributed to Villa's anger and frustration over the United States government choosing to back Villa's northern Mexico rival Carranza. What really set off Villa's reprisal against defenseless Columbus was his desire for revenge. He had been cheated by an arms dealer who sold the revolutionary general blank movie ammunition. The arms dealer happened to be out of town at the time of the raid and escaped Villa's vengeance.

Indian Emily, Fact or Fiction?

A Love Story From the Frontier

IT'S ONLY PROPER that stories from the frontier be truthful, and my hat is off to the folks at Fort Davis in far West Texas for setting the record straight on Indian Emily, despite the fact that their action has ruined a wonderful love story.

As many travelers to Fort Davis know, Indian Emily was the young Apache girl who is supposed to have saved the post—Fort Davis—from surprise attack when she alerted her lover, a young army lieutenant, that the hostiles were coming. The state of Texas erected a historical marker to her memory in 1936, and the love story-adventure was written up by several people, including Fort Davis's distinguished historian Barry Scobee, who even reiterated the words that Emily is said to have uttered to a fort sentry just before she died.

Through the years, Indian Emily's story has been a central theme surrounding a number of activities held in the West Texas community. The story has helped attract many tourists to the fort and also indirectly helped draw attention to restoring the fort buildings and ruins during early years of preservation.

Unfortunately, the story is not true but merely a legend, say fort historians. Thus, Indian Emily's historic marker located in the old fort cemetery has been removed for storage in the fort's archives.

Since Indian Emily's story was first published in Carl Raht's wonderful book *The Romance of the Davis Mountains and the Big Bend Country* in 1919, the tale of the Indian girl's romance with the army officer has been published throughout the country and has been featured in films, television, books, magazines, and newspapers. The story goes something like this:

Emily, an Apache maiden, was wounded and captured by troopers out of Fort Davis in the late 1860s. She was taken to the fort where she was nursed back to health by a Mrs. Eason. The Indian girl grew up on the post and eventually fell in love with Mrs. Eason's son, Lieutenant Tom Eason. When the soldier married a girl of his own race, Indian Emily was heartbroken and returned to her Apache tribe. Later, as the story goes, she over-hears a plan for an Apache assault on the fort. In an act of selfless love, she slips away in the middle of the night to warn the young offi-cer, Eason. As she approaches the fort, a nervous sentry shoots her when she fails to answer his challenge. She dies in the arms of Mrs. Eason after telling of her everlasting love for her son and of the impending attack on the fort. She was buried in the post cemetery, and the marker that was erected by the state was placed on what was identified as her gravestone.

According to Raht and Scobee, the story had been confirmed in 1917 by Henry Flipper, the first African-American to graduate from West Point. Flipper served for a time at Fort Davis and Fort Concho but left the army after being court-martialed for allegedly stealing money from the Fort Davis commissary. Flipper later went on to be a successful mining engineer and leading citizen of El Paso.

After lots of research, fort historians found that no Apache attack was ever planned or carried out. Also, the researchers found that there was never a Lieutenant Tom Eason assigned duty at the fort, and no person by that name ever served in the U.S. Army prior to 1903.

Historians have found additional flaws in the story as well, includ-ing the fact that Emily did not behave like an Apache woman, and that Apache women never took part in any attack or did any fighting except in dire circumstances.

One historian's theory is the story was generated by someone "reading Victorian romances," and it was passed along as a true event.

Even though historians are now sure that such an event never took place and that there was never an Indian Emily, some quietly admit that "we can't prove it didn't happen, either."

The late great Texas folklorist J. Frank Dobie used to have a say-ing about such stories. "Perhaps it didn't happen that way, but it should have." The story of Indian Emily is still an enchanting one like many others about events that have taken place in our state.

Clay Wyatt, Cowboy Philosopher

Eighty-Seven-Year-Old Pen Pal Man of Integrity

IN LATE FEBRUARY 1997, sad news came to me in a telephone call from Tilden, a small community south of San Antonio. My eighty-seven-year-old pen pal, Clay Wyatt, had died unexpectedly that Monday afternoon. His family told me that death came quietly and swiftly while he sat writing another of his many newsy letters.

It's been a long time since my friend Clay died, but I still miss getting his letters because each was filled with love for his family, his grandchildren for whom he was justly proud, the livestock that he was no longer able to ride, herd, or wrangle, and for his pen pal friends scattered near and far.

I kept each of Clay's letters, and they nearly fill a file cabinet drawer. It is amazing how many he wrote me over the span of some two and a half years. What is even more unusual about our relationship is he never really told me how he got my name and address and what spurred him on to communicate with me so often. We spoke a couple of times on the telephone, but mostly our communicating was through the U.S. mail.

Clay had a wonderful way of expressing himself. He told me in one of his letters that when he is alone and has nothing to do but think of the "good ol' times," he uses that time "in scribbling." I am so proud that he chose me as a person to send his scribbling to because I have gathered a great deal of knowledge from my friend.

Clay's letters would range in length from eight to ten pages, and I have received several twice that length. Each was carefully written in longhand and laced with some grand stories about horses, mules, his short career as a semiprofessional baseball player, hauling a baby elephant to Waco without pay, trucking honey bees to Louisiana, and delivering bat manure from a cave in Hays County to an irrigated farm at Crystal City.

Perhaps the most revealing thing about Clay's letters was that he was a man of integrity, and he did not mind sharing with me some of his lessons from life.

"If you make a vow or

promise, live up to it," Clay wrote, describing a lecture he got from his father while still a "young button."

"If you have trouble making that promise stick, don't dodge the man but walk right up to him and tell him you will do your best to fulfill it. Look the man right in the eye and tell him... Don't send him the word."

Another letter brought this advice, also passed along from his father: A person that betrays a man's confidence is the lowest kind to ever squat between two boot heels. Never burn, beg, or steal. There's someone you can turn to and he will always see that you don't walk away hungry."

In another letter, Clay described to me the death of his longtime friend Dick Shelton, who died in a Cotulla hospital.

"I was sitting on the side of his bed. He told me that he was glad that I had come to see him. As we were talking old times he turned his head to the other side of the bed and rode over the last ridge. He and my dad both rode off holding my hand. My dad died back in the early 1920s, and Dick made it to 1970. It hurts me to remember them that way."

According to Clay's son, my friend died with his writing pen in his hand. The letter he was writing was directed to me.

I thought about that letter Clay had written to me about the passing of his dad and of his friend Dick Shelton. I wish I could have been there to hold his hand as he "rode over the ridge."

I never had the opportunity to meet Clay Wyatt personally and to shake his hand, but he was the kind of man I would have been proud to sit with on the porch and talk about cows, horses, mules, dogs, and other simple things in life. We both enjoyed writing about our times in the country, listening to the squeak of the windmills as they turn in the wind, hearing the gurgling of the water coming up the pipe as it flows into the storage tank, and the songbirds entertaining us from the nearby grove of trees.

When my time comes to "cross over the ridge," I expect to find Clay Wyatt at the gate with an outstretched hand. He will have things all lined out on God's home range.

The Concho Country Had Its Bad Boys

*Cherokee Bill, the Ketchums,
and others were among the worst*

THE CONCHO COUNTRY OF WESTERN TEXAS has provided the Southwest with some of its very worst outlaws with bunches of notches on their guns, and much of the violence of the 1880s and 1890s was as senseless then as what is happening today on our streets and in our schools.

Most often, like today, the violence came when hotheaded young men had disagreements over women, money, or wagers or when they got extra brave and tough while drinking liquor or took offense to something said by another. Like today, these turn-of-the-century hoodlums were armed to the teeth. The only difference is today's young toughs have more firepower.

Social development experts say history repeats itself, and today's bloody violence certainly mirrors what happened in the frontier towns of a century ago. There was a lot of blood spilled in those days before tough lawmen and judges started making the criminals respect them, because it could become unhealthy and at times downright deadly for them to ignore law and order.

One of the worst of the bunch was Crawford Goldsby, better known as Cherokee Bill, who was born at Fort Concho on February 8, 1876, and who died dangling from a hangman's noose at Fort Smith, Arkansas, on March 17, 1896. He was barely twenty years old.

Goldsby, who made outlaw history in Indian Territory, now Oklahoma, was the son of St. George and Ellen Beck Goldsby. The elder Goldsby was a soldier in the 10th U.S. Cavalry and claimed to be of black, Sioux, Mexican, and white ancestry. Bill's mother was reportedly half black, one quarter white, and one quarter Cherokee Indian.

By the time young Goldsby was seven, his parents had separated. He moved from Fort Concho, at present-day San Angelo, with his mother to Fort Gibson, Indian Territory, and later attended a school for

Indians in Cherokee, Kansas, for three years. He also attended the Carlisle Industrial School for Indians at Carlisle, Pennsylvania, for two years, yet some sources say that despite this education, Cherokee Bill could barely read or write.

According to his biographers, Cherokee Bill had a sister, Maude, and she was the reason that Cherokee Bill became a wanted man. He killed her husband, George Brown, in 1894. Brown was just one of six people who died during that year after getting crossways with the hot-tempered Goldsby.

The young Goldsby ran away from home and as a teenager got involved with a gang of thieves and rustlers led by Jim and Bill Cook. While riding with the Cook gang, Cherokee Bill shot and killed lawman Sequoyah Houston at 14 Mile Creek, near Tahlequah, Indian Territory. The Cooks had been chased by a posse of lawmen who had a warrant for Jim Cook's arrest for theft. A gunfight broke out when the gang refused to surrender.

Always on the go, Cherokee Bill got into another scrape at a dance being held at Fort Gibson. In a fistfight with Jake Lewis, the young outlaw got a thrashing. Rather than run to lick his wounds, Bill pulled his revolver and shot Lewis in the stomach. Although he was seriously wounded, Lewis was lucky and survived. Others did not.

Not long after having the scrape with Lewis and shooting him, Cherokee Bill killed his brother-in-law, George Brown, after he learned that Brown had severely beaten his wife, Maude, the young

> According to his biographers, Cherokee Bill had a sister, Maude, and she was the reason that Cherokee Bill became a wanted man. He killed her husband, George Brown, in 1894. Brown was just one of six people who died during

gunman's sister. After the slaying, Cherokee Bill escaped prosecution by hiding out in the Indian Territory back country.

Goldsby, or Cherokee Bill, was now a wanted man. His violent temper erupted on a train ride when Conductor Sam Collins threatened to throw him off the train for misbehaving. Cherokee Bill shot Collins dead then got off the train at the next stop and vanished. He also marked up another victim who worked for the railroad in 1894. During an attempted robbery of a train station, Goldsby shot and killed the station agent, Dick Richards.

The elusive Goldsby was finally brought to justice after he was caught visiting his sweetheart. He was charged and tried for murder and sentenced to be hanged in connection with the slaying of

that year after getting crossways with the hot-tempered Goldsby.

The young Goldsby ran away from home and as a teenager got involved with a gang of thieves and rustlers led by Jim and Bill Cook.

store clerk Ernest Melton at Lenapah, Oklahoma. Melton was shot in the head during the robbery of the Shufeldt and Son General Store.

Although he was tried and convicted in the court of Judge Isaac Parker at Fort Smith, Arkansas, Goldsby's defense attorney, J. Warren Reed, found ways to appeal the conviction, thus keeping Goldsby from the gallows.

However, on July 26, 1895, he attempted to escape jail at Fort Smith and killed a guard, Lawrence Keating, the father of four young children. Another prisoner talked Goldsby into surrendering because he could not get out of jail without being shot down by lawmen who quickly surrounded the place.

Goldsby's surrender after the jailbreak attempt did not deter Judge Parker from quickly sentencing him to hang at the conclusion of his second trial, and defense attorney Reed could not appeal the second conviction. The youthful killer, with seven or more killings to his credit, was hanged on March 17, 1896, less than a month after his twentieth birthday.

When asked if he wished to make a last statement before dropping through the gallows' trapdoor, Goldsby was arrogant to the end, telling the hangman: "No, I came here to die, not to make a speech."

It's said that the crowd of official witnesses at Goldsby's execution cheered loudly when the killer reached the end of his rope. Justice was more swift and less forgiving in those days.

Judge Parker characterized Cherokee Bill as a "bloodthirsty mad dog who killed for the love of killing" and as "the most vicious" of all the outlaws in the Oklahoma Territory.

After his death, his mother took his body to the Fort Gibson area where he is buried in the Cherokee National Cemetery.

Although Cherokee Bill spent most of his hell-raising days north of the Red River, other gunmen of national reputation with roots to the Concho country also made news throughout the Southwest with killings, bank robberies, train holdups, and other mischief.

Desperado Dave Atkins, who was able to keep a fairly low profile during his outlaw days, evaded justice and capture for more than twenty years, but he finally went to the state prison in Huntsville for killing a man in a Knickerbocker saloon argument.

Not much is known about Dave Atkins' early life in and around San Angelo and Tom Green County. He did work as a cowboy from time to time, and among his friends were the Ketchum brothers and several members of the Wild Bunch, including Will Carver, Ben Kilpatrick, Ed Cullen, and others who were adept at robbing trains.

Atkins was born in May 1874 in Tom Green County and lived with his family in the Knickerbocker community, then a thriving ranching community. He was a good-looking man with dark gray eyes and black hair. He was nearly six feet tall and appeared to have a good life ahead of him before getting mixed up with outlaw friends.

Atkins, then twenty years old, was implicated in the murder of John N. "Jap" Powers in the late fall of 1895. Powers had a ranch neighboring the Ketchums just south of Knickerbocker. The Ketchums were known to have bad reputations, and there were reports that the Ketchums had had "words" with Powers. On December 12 Powers was shot to death in a pasture while trying to catch a saddle horse. Three bullets struck him in the back and a fourth bullet split his skull open. Lawmen immediately suspected Tom Ketchum, Dave Atkins, and Bud Upshaw as being involved in the crime.

Fearing arrest, Upshaw and Atkins struck out for Arizona. Ketchum fled to New Mexico where he hoped to join his brother,

Sam Ketchum, who was working in the Pecos Valley country. Will Carver, then a rider with the Butch Cassidy Wild Bunch, joined Atkins and Upshaw in Cochise County, Arizona.

In 1896 the three men were indicted by a Tom Green County grand jury for the killing of Powers, but the charges were later dropped against the trio when it was learned that Mrs. Powers and the ranch foreman had killed the old man. Despite the charges being dropped, Atkins had been branded an outlaw.

On March 20, 1897, Atkins and Tom Hardin got into an argument while drinking beer at the Brown Saloon in Knickerbocker. According to a newspaper account, Atkins and a friend, Sam Moore, were drinking prior to going to a Mexican dance. Hardin, a Knickerbocker merchant, spoke critically of the men for shooting their pistols into the air, saying one of the bullets fired had just missed his head. Atkins, hot-tempered and glassy-eyed from the six or more drinks he had consumed, turned on Hardin, saying: "Damn you. You struck me over the head once with an axe handle."

Hardin denied ever hitting Atkins. As a result, Atkins called Hardin a liar, pulled his pistol, and shot Hardin twice in the head. Atkins left the shooting scene and headed west. He was finally caught in Montana after taking part in several train robberies with the Ketchum gang.

In March 1900 Tom Green County sheriff Rhome Shields traveled to Butte, Montana, and returned Atkins to San Angelo to stand trial for Hardin's slaying. Atkins said he wanted to see his wife and child in San Angelo, but the sheriff had to tell him that his wife had divorced him and married another man.

In May 1901 Atkins jumped bail and fled before being brought to trial. He roamed the world before returning to San Angelo in 1919 at which time he surrendered to the sheriff. He stood trial for the Hardin slaying and got a five-year prison sentence.

During a part of the time he wandered the world, Atkins joined the Canadian amy and fought in World War I. He was discharged a first lieutenant. He also was in the British army during the Boer War in South Africa.

After serving time in the state prison, Atkins returned to Knickerbocker where he lived quietly until he was arrested on an assault charge in 1932. Apparently the charge was dismissed when Atkins was admitted to the Wichita Falls State Hospital where he remained a ward of the state until his death on June 12, 1964, at the age of ninety-three. He had spent thirty-one years, ten months, and one day in the state hospital.

According to Pinkerton Detective Agency records, Atkins was involved in three major train robberies, including the heist of some $42,000 in the robbery of the Southern Pacific train at Lozier in Terrell County between Dryden and Langtry on May 14, 1896.

Tom and Sam Ketchum had reputations as troublemakers while growing up in the Knickerbocker area. Another of the Ketchums—Berry—was a well-respected rancher and horse breeder who attempted to help his brothers straighten out their lives, but without success. When his brother Tom "Black Jack" Ketchum was awaiting the hangman's noose in Clayton, New Mexico, Berry Ketchum made the tedious trip from San Angelo to visit him in the Clayton jail. However, tough man Tom refused to see him. Berry left some spending money for Tom with the New Mexico jailer and returned home.

When the Ketchums left the Concho country after the slaying of Jap Powers, the men hit the "hoot owl trail" in New Mexico and Arizona. Tom Ketchum told friends that he was going to join up with Butch Cassidy and the "Hole-In-The-Wall Gang" or "Wild Bunch." Although the Ketchums never officially were members of the gang, they did know Cassidy, the Sundance Kid, Will Carver, and Harvey Logan as well.

Eventually the Ketchum brothers stopped stealing cattle and started robbing stores and post offices. Soon they graduated to robbing trains. Their first train robbery was of the SP train at Lozier, where they got the $42,000. This first train holdup proved to be so easy the Ketchums decided to stick with the plan. It proved lucrative until Tom Ketchum attempted to rob a train by himself at Folsum, New Mexico, in 1897. His brother Sam had recently died in prison of blood poisoning from a gangrenous wound in his arm suffered in a gunfight with railroad detectives some months earlier.

When he stopped the train at Folsum, Black Jack found that trainman Frank Harrington was prepared. When he opened the express car door on Black Jack's command, Harrington shot the bandit with a shotgun. Ketchum fell from the car into a ditch, then dragged himself away. He was found the following day near death by another train crew. His right arm was eventually amputated at San Rafael, New Mexico.

After a long, slow, painful recovery, Black Jack was put in jail to await trial. He was found guilty and sentenced to hang.

On April 26, 1901, Tom "Black Jack" Ketchum climbed the gallows steps. He had requested a fiddler play some music for him. He did not appear to be fearful of his fate. His hanging was not pleasant. It was marred by the fact that the noose decapitated him instead of breaking his neck. When Ketchum's 200-pound body went through the trapdoor, his head was yanked free from his body and tumbled down among the spectators. It was a gruesome sight.

Ketchum was buried in Clayton, but his burial place was relocated about thirty-two years later when the town platted another burial ground. When his grave was opened for removal and relocation, observers said the interior of Ketchum's coffin was in relatively good condition. Ketchum's jet-black hair and mustache were still visible, but had turned maroon red. The black burial suit was discolored, but the coat sleeve was still neatly folded over the stump of his right arm that had been shattered by Frank Harrington's shotgun blast.

There has been some speculation that Black Jack Ketchum did not die on the gallows, but there is adequate proof that he did. It was a terrible end for a cowboy gone wrong.

Ben Kilpatrick and Will Carver, two West Texas outlaws who appeared in the famous group portrait of the Wild Bunch taken by a Fort Worth photographer, met earlier while working as cowboys in the Knickerbocker area. Although their outlaw activities took them all over the great Southwest and to the Canadian border, they would return to Texas to die.

About the time that Black Jack Ketchum was choosing his life's work of robbing, Kilpatrick and Carver were arriving in the San Angelo area. Carver, a quiet and unassuming man, was from the Bandera area in the Texas Hill Country. Kilpatrick was from nearby Concho County, having grown up on a stock farm between Eden and Paint Rock.

The lure of gambling, or perhaps just the sporting way of life, was appealing to all the Concho County boys. Ketchum, in particular, liked to gamble and at one time won some $3,000. However, he claimed the money was his "inheritance." When it was gone, he returned to Texas from Arizona and joined up with Kilpatrick and Carver. These three were the core of the Black Jack Ketchum gang that rustled cattle, stole horses, robbed post offices and stores, and in general, kept the gentle folk uneasy and upset.

The gang soured on Tom Ketchum's leadership and split up before Ketchum made the mistake of his life trying to rob a train by himself. Carver and Kilpatrick went their separate ways.

Ben Kilpatrick, called the "Tall Texan" by the Pinkertons and others seeking the elusive outlaw, joined the Butch Cassidy gang after splitting away from Ketchum. After taking part in a train robbery in Montana in 1901, he was captured in St. Louis along with his girlfriend, Laura Bullion. Laura was also from the Knickerbocker community in Texas and had worked several train holdups with Kilpatrick and Will Carver. Kilpatrick was tried for his part in the Montana robbery and sentenced to fifteen years in federal prison. He was released after serving ten and a half years.

During the time Kilpatrick was in jail for the Montana robbery, Carver returned to Texas and made a visit to the Kilpatrick place in Concho County. While there, a dispute erupted when a neighbor accused the Kilpatricks of allowing their hogs to run on his place. The accusations grew heated and tempers were hot. It resulted in gunplay, with the complainant, O. G. Thornton, being shot with a rifle. Carver is suspected of being the shootist. Knowing that the law would be quick to convict them if they stayed around, Carver and

Kilpatrick's brother, George, fled on horseback.

On April 2, 1901, Carver and George Kilpatrick were in Sonora buying supplies. They had been reported in the area, and lawmen suspected them of planning to rob the Sonora bank.

Sutton County sheriff E. S. Briant had been informed a few days earlier that two men were being sought for the Thornton slaying in Concho County. The description gave Briant reason to believe that the same men had been in Sonora some six weeks earlier.

About 9 o'clock that night, Deputy Sharp was notified by his brother, "Boosie" Sharp, that two men were in the bakery trying to buy grain for their horses. Sharp told the sheriff, who quickly got additional help from his other deputy, Davis, and Constable W. D. Thomason.

The lawmen entered the store and told the men they were under arrest. Kilpatrick, standing closest to the door, made an attempt to draw his pistol, and at the same time Carver pulled his gun as well. Sheriff Briant shot Carver before he could cock the pistol, and Constable Thomason shot Kilpatrick. Immediately, each of the officers fired several shots at the two men as they fell to the floor. Carver was shot through the right lung, the ball traveling through his body and lodging against his spine. He also was hit twice in the right arm, twice in the right leg, and once in the temple. He lived about three hours after being shot.

Kilpatrick had a wound in the left breast, two shots in the left arm, one in the knee, and a glancing ball struck him in the left forehead. Despite the seriousness of his wounds, Kilpatrick would survive. On April 27, 1901, twenty-five days after the bakery shootout, George Kilpatrick was put under $4,000 bond for the murder of Thornton during a habeas corpus hearing in Paint Rock, Concho County.

Ben Kilpatrick, the last of the Wild Bunch, was to die in a botched train robbery on March 13, 1912, when he and another man, Ole Hobeck, a former prison mate, tried to rob the Galveston, Harrisburg and San Antonio Railroad Train No. 9 east of Sanderson in Terrell County. Express guard David A. Trousdale smashed Kilpatrick's skull with an ice mallet when he tried to enter the express car. Hobeck was shot to death.

The only person to realize any benefits from these bandits was Sheriff E. S. Briant of Sutton County, Sonora, who received $1,000 reward for the capture of one of the Black Jack Ketchum gang—Will Carver. Superintendent G. A. Taft of the Wells Fargo Express Company made the announcement. "This reward is in lieu of the standing reward of $300 offered for the arrest and conviction," said Taft.

Carver's belongings were sold to the highest bidder at a public auction in Sonora in early July 1901. His dun horse brought $40, his bay horse brought $65, a young sorrel horse sold for $60, and a brown horse brought $55. Carver's silver-mounted six-shooter sold for $32.50, his gold watch brought $30, a five-shooter pistol sold for $6, and his diamond ring brought $125.

The Earl of Aylesford

NOBODY REALLY KNOWS why an English peer was in Big Spring, but he seems to have left Merry Ol' England under some cloud of suspicion.

Joseph Heneage Finch, the Earl of Alyesford, was just one of several English noblemen to come to western Texas in the late 1800s where they established ranches or businesses. Two members of the English gentry, William "Billy" Anson, the third Earl of Lichfield, and Lord Godfrey J. B. Chetwynd made their home in the immediate San Angelo area. The mustachioed Finch was the best known because of his eccentric behavior.

The Earl of Aylesford could be described as a tenderfoot on the Texas range, but he was no stranger to good horses, firearms, hunting dogs, or good food, and he was particularly fond of good whiskey. He also never refused "a bit of" gin, brandy, or wine.

Born in 1849 in Packington Hall in Warwickshire, Finch left England at the age of twenty-nine to rebuild his fortune and to escape the scandal of a very nasty divorce. According to some informants, Finch was serving in the British army, and while he was away on a campaign in some remote part of the world, his wife found someone else. Things got so bad that a divorce was the only suitable solution to a sticky situation. He quickly packed his bags—some say more than fifty pieces of luggage—gathered all the cash he could, and left for New York. There he met the railroad magnate Jay Gould, who financed construction of the Texas and Pacific Railroad that extends across Texas from east to west. Big Spring would become a major T&P railroad stop.

Finch, a robust man with a quick smile and hearty laugh, was a typical English nobleman. He had been educated at Cambridge and was a very close friend of the Prince of Wales, who later became King Edward VII. Finch had accompanied the prince on a special hunting trip to India and owned several custom-made rifles and shotguns given to him by the prince. If

Finch were given a choice of meeting a feisty young woman or going hunting, he would quickly accept the latter.

Finch asked his friend Jay Gould the whereabouts of the

Above: *The Earl of Aylesford, "tenderfoot." Photo courtesy Big Spring Heritage Museum.*

wildest parts of America. He wanted to visit the area and hunt buffalo, antelope, deer, and other game. Gould told him to travel to southwestern Texas. His trip was over when he reached Colorado City where he met Texas Ranger John Birdwell, who became his friend and helped him find suitable acreage for ranching. The Earl, as he liked to be called, arrived in Colorado City in 1883, where he visited with rancher D. C. Earnest. Earnest later described the earl in a letter that he wrote to Mrs. Mabel Cooper, who resided in Edinburg, Texas.

During the winter of 1883-84, Finch came to the Earnest ranch to hunt.

"He was a big, fine looking fellow, about 6 feet 4 inches tall," Earnest wrote. The earl was dressed in English riding clothes and riding a "muley" saddle, one without a horn. He told Earnest that he had seen lots of antelope but had not been able to "bag one."

The morning was cool, Earnest noted, and the earl pulled from his coat a flask of whiskey. He offered it to the Texan then took a good swallow. Earnest saddled one of his best ponies, got his Winchester, and the men headed out across the open country. As soon as the earl saw the grazing herd of antelope, he shouldered his rifle and fired but missed. Earnest said the same thing happened several times that day.

The next morning when the men went out hunting, Earnest told the earl to be patient and wait until they could get closer to the game before shooting. The earl followed Earnest's instructions and got several antelope that day. The two men became close friends after those days of hunting, and Earnest helped the earl in getting settled into the ranching business after he bought several sections of land south of Big Spring.

While not a substantial contributor to a rapidly developing section of the country, Finch became a legend in his own time. Sporting a top hat and corduroy britches, his look drew lots of attention and conversation among the settlers.

When the earl arrived in Big Spring with his entourage of servants, hunting dogs, horses, and a baggage car filled with luggage, he had no place to stay. When the operator of the Cosmopolitan Hotel attempted to turn him away, the earl simply asked, "How much" for the place. The owner gave an astronomical figure. The earl bought it without argument. Although he later sold the hotel back to its original owner, he always had a permanent place to rest when he came to town from the ranch. He also bought a meat market when he could not get the right cut of steak, and he purchased a saloon in order to always have the right amount and the right brand of whiskey on hand.

The Earl of Aylesford became a distinguished resident of Big Spring, and local society (what there was of it) welcomed him with open arms. He declined all invitations, however, preferring to share drinks with the cowboys, ranchers, card sharks, and others who hung out at the saloons. At times he would be his own bartender, serving drinks to both friend and stranger alike for as long as the liquor held out.

The night he took a notion to own a saloon, he paid $6,000 for the place—much more than it was worth—and invited everyone in town to step up to the bar and have a drink on the house, or as many drinks as you could hold before falling down. The party went on all night and into the next day. The town has never seen such a party since.

His three-section ranch, located about twelve miles south of Big Spring, soon became a very popular place among the cowboys and their employers. His ranch house, a story and a half high, had nine rooms opening off a wide hallway constructed down the middle of the house. The earl's West Texas castle was nothing like the mansions he knew about in England. His castle was of unpainted boards, and there were so many guns on the walls it bristled like a fortress.

As soon as the earl was settled in on his place, his two brothers, Daniel and Clement, arrived for an extended visit. They brought along five servants, twenty horses, and a coach and a dogcart, neither of which any western Texas resident had ever seen.

According to various historians who tracked the Earl of Aylesford's activities, he never appeared ready to get into the cattle business. However, he did have a very large horse barn and a fenced dog run. One of the most impressive monuments left on his ranch was a pile of whiskey bottles said to be as large as a haystack.

Noted for drinking up to two quarts of whiskey a day, it was obvious that the earl intended to drink himself to death. He soon did after living it up in Big Spring for four years.

One night just before Christmas in 1885, Finch, the Earl of Aylesford, threw a huge party at the Cosmopolitan Hotel. Everyone in town was invited and whiskey flowed like water.

During the party, the earl rose from the chair where he was sitting and called for the attention of everyone.

"Good-bye, boys," he said in a quiet tone of voice. Then he dropped dead at the ripe age of thirty-six.

According to several stories passed along from those wild and woolly days, there is a footnote to the Earl of Aylesford's life and times in Texas.

In order to prepare the earl's body for shipment back to England, a noted Dallas undertaker was contacted and soon arrived on the train. The undertaker and the earl's physician removed his vital organs and filled the body cavity with charcoal and chalk. The "innards" were put in a bucket for disposal. While no one was watching, the earl's pet bear, which lived outside the hotel and had accompanied the earl to the nearby saloon, found the bucket and had himself a snack. When citizens learned of the bear's last supper, the faultless animal was taken to a nearby stand of trees and hanged.

Although Finch had never really contributed anything worthwhile to his adopted community, he was to be honored nearly 100 years later with a historical marker in his memory, and a street was named for him.

After his death in 1885, the administrator of his estate learned that the earl died with only $750 to his name. He had squandered thousands of pounds annually during his short stay in America. His obituary commanded space in the *Chicago Herald* and the *Fort Worth Gazette* as well as the *Big Spring Pantagraph*.

Although Finch is remembered

> He also bought a meat market when he could not get the right cut of steak, and he purchased a saloon in order to always have the right amount and the right brand of whiskey on hand.

Left: *Billy Anson, 3rd Earl of Lichfield. Photo courtesy West Texas Collection, ASU.*

for his eccentric behavior, the two other Englishmen made solid contributions to their adopted West Texas homeland.

William "Billy" Anson, the third Earl of Lichfield, who was born and reared in Staffordshire, England, came to Texas in the 1880s and established a ranch with his two brothers, Claud and Frank.

After a short time the brothers decided to return to England, but "Billy" chose to stay and get into the horse business. An accomplished horseman and polo player, Anson bred a fine string of horses that became known all over the Southwest. In 1902 he moved to Tom Green County and purchased the Head of the River Ranch near

Christoval on the headwaters of the South Concho River. Anson was commissioned by the British government to provide horses to the British army during the Boer War. The animals were shipped direct to Capetown, South Africa, from the port of Galveston. Anson served as an officer during World War I and married Louise Van Wagenen in New York in 1917. The couple lived on the ranch until 1923 when they returned to England where Anson died in 1926. His ranch continues in the family to this day.

Lord Godfrey came to Texas as a young boy from his native

Right: *J. B. Chetwynd, Lord Godfrey. Photo courtesy* San Angelo Standard-Times.

England and grew up working on sheep and cattle ranches between Menard and Eden. He assisted in the surveying of a number of counties in western Texas and gained a reputation as a fine camp cook.

In the 1880s Lord Godfrey came to San Angelo, working on survey crews, and assisted surveyor H. B. Tarver in laying out the town of San Angelo. During World War I, Lord Godfrey returned to England where he became a noted figure in the munitions business. He was the head of the Vickers steel mill for ten years and proposed radical changes in the production of artillery shells.

After the war was over, Lord Godfrey returned to San Angelo where his interest in minerals consumed much of his time. He is remembered by old-timers for his regular tea-time routine each afternoon when he would come into San Angelo's swankiest hotel, the Cactus, accompanied by his dog, Ferach. He was the only guest ever allowed to bring a pet into the hotel dining room where he would give the dog a piece of bread dunked into tea for good behavior.

During one of his many excursions looking for minerals in Central Texas, Lord Godfrey got pneumonia and died. He was seventy-three. Of the three Englishmen, only Lord Godfrey is buried in Texas soil. A simple headstone marks his gravesite in San Angelo's Fairmount Cemetery.

The History of Aviation

THE HISTORY OF AVIATION is believed by many to have had its earliest beginnings in the Texas Hill Country, but proof of flight by an airship created and constructed by a Luckenbach schoolteacher is hard to come by. A national aviation magazine has been curious about the mystery.

Many folks in the hills about Fredericksburg believe Jacob Freidrich Brodbent made the first manned flight in an airship thirty-eight years before the Wright Brothers, Orville and Wilbur, got their craft into the air at Kitty Hawk. If Brodbent flew his contraption at treetop level in a field outside San Antonio in August 1865, there are few solid records to back it up.

The mystery has been featured in *Aviation History Magazine*, as well as other publications over the years. Still, there remains little information about Brodbent's deed, if he in fact made such a flight.

Despite the support of descendants of the German immigrant-teacher-inventor, historians Jay Miller and Roger Bilstein, authors of the book *Aviation In Texas: An Illustrated History*, say that Brodbent could not have gotten his spring-powered airship off the ground.

However, there are early-day reports from witnesses and stories in old newspapers that support Brodbent's claim to flying, although his primitive craft crashed because he had not perfected a way to rewind the clock-like spring as it unwound.

Walter Edwards of Fredericksburg, a local historian and for years associated with the Fredericksburg Chamber of Commerce, states in his book *Tales of Old Fredericksburg* that original sketches of Brodbent's airship and other documents about the venture have been lost or destroyed. However, sufficient data has been collected to authenticate the fact that Brodbent had projected his theory that man could fly in a flying machine and that such a vehicle could be constructed.

In the 1960s a San Angelo reporter interviewed some of Brodbent's descendants and others who remembered seeing pieces of Brodbent's cedar and canvas airplane in the loft of a barn at Luckenbach. The barn later burned to the ground.

Brodbent's granddaughter, Mrs. Staudt, told the reporter that she could remember her grandfather but that she was too young to understand the "many things that he had done." Brodbent's secrets to his airship invention and his work were buried with him, she said.

"They always said that my grandmother was so disgusted with him for wasting all that time and money on the airplane that when he died she went down and threw it [the airplane] into the creek," she told the reporter. Perhaps metal parts from America's first flying machine are beneath the water and mud of Grape Creek.

According to information collected by historian Edwards, Brodbent built a model of the spring-powered airplane in 1863 and followed it up with a series of refined designs: "Brodbent's toys were a source of amusement for Fredericksburg citizens," Edwards wrote.

In 1865 Brodbent advertised in a San Antonio newspaper an appeal to raise funds to construct his flying machine. A wealthy physician, Dr. Ferdinand Herff, was one of his principal backers.

When Brodbent finished making his airplane, he invited Herff and others to witness the first flight to be conducted in a meadow outside of San Antonio. A crowd gathered, the craft was made ready, and Brodbent piloted the strange-looking craft over a short distance before crashing. The

Walter Edwards of Fredericksburg, a local historian and for years associated with the Fredericksburg Chamber of Commerce, states in his book *Tales of Old Fredericksburg* that original sketches of Brodbent's airship and other documents about the venture

inventor wasn't hurt, but the airplane suffered more than just cracked and crumpled wings. The investors were shattered as well, Edwards reported in his book.

According to another source, Brodbent did not give up on his idea about flight. He traveled the country making talks and showing his designs and drawings. Despite his efforts, he was never able to get adequate support or funding to follow up his ideas.

In failing health, Brodbent retired to his Luckenbach farm and gave up soliciting for funds for his airplane invention in 1893 when he was seventy-two years old. He died at the age of eighty-eight and is buried in a small cemetery off the Sisterdale Road near Fredericksburg.

Brodbent was among the first have been lost or destroyed. However, sufficient data has been collected to authenticate the fact that Brodbent had projected his theory that man could fly in a flying machine and that such a vehicle could be constructed.

German immigrants to reach the Texas Hill Country. He arrived in Fredericksburg in March 1847, and after farming for a brief time he became the second schoolteacher in the Vereins Kirche. He also taught in rural schools, including South Grape Creek and Luckenbach.

Mrs. Staudt recalled to reporters a number of years ago about hearing stories of her grandfather telling his students that someday man would fly like the birds. Perhaps Jacob Brodbent should get more credit than history books have given him.

Aviation has fascinated Texans for generations. The greatest adventure in aviation is credited to the Wright Brothers—or perhaps Jacob Brodbent—but a Menard farmer isn't too far behind. J. H. Dunagan made his own airplane then flew it without the benefit of instruction. In fact, he soloed the first time he flew his machine.

Dunagan was a man who just naturally liked building things. He got the itch to build his own airplane in 1919 and got the plans for the airplane from the Heath Aircraft Company. For power, Dunagan ordered a four-cylinder Henderson motorcycle engine that was converted for airplane use. The fuselage was made of a framework of steel tubing, covered with Irish linen. Dope was put on the linen to make it tight and waterproof. The propeller was ordered from a Fort Worth company, and the wheels of the airplane were adapted from motorcycle use.

After Dunagan had assembled

the plane, he decided to taxi the aircraft around a field on the Robert Flutsch place. He said he never intended to fly the plane, but while the craft taxied about the field, going faster and faster, all of a sudden the ground slipped away and he was airborne. Having read some books on flying, he tried to remember the tips listed in the books. He successfully landed the plane, but he never attempted to fly it again.

However, news of his feat quickly spread. A man named Kelly McLain of Melvin came over and did an interview about the experience. Soon people from all over Central Texas were coming to his place to see the plane and to have their photos taken in it or beside it. Several people tried the plane out, taxiing around the place and running into the fences, breaking the propeller. He finally sold the plane to some men from Eden. He never knew what happened to it after that.

Another Texan, John Valentine Pliska, a Midland blacksmith, constructed an airplane in 1912. It had the appearance of a Wright machine. The airplane was later restored by George T. Abell, and it is now housed at Midland International Airport.

Raindrops Keep Falling on My Head

Droughts Bring Out the Rainmakers

A HALF CENTURY AGO most of Texas was gripped in one of the worst droughts on record. Despite an occasional cloud overhead drifting by from time to time, rain just would not come. People were getting desperate.

Otis Cox of Brady recalled the drought vividly. Cox, a longtime friend and former automotive repair shop owner, was called "the rainmaker" by his friends and acquaintances in Brady. They had a reason. He was working with the country's top rainmaker, Dr. Irving P. Krick of Denver, Colorado.

"I never made it rain," Cox said. "All I did was operate the cloud seeding apparatus."

In the 1950s drought, farmers and ranchers and business leaders were deeply concerned about the water supplies and getting adequate rain to grow crops and grass to feed cattle and sheep.

Dr. I. P. Krick, known as the "Rainmaker of the Rockies," was a widely known weather forecaster who started a water resources development firm in Denver after the end of World War II. Krick gained notoriety while serving in the army as the official weatherman for General Dwight D. Eisenhower. It was Krick's job to select the best day for launching the invasion of Normandy, and he picked D-Day, the 6th of June, as the best time to assault the beaches.

Cox said Krick's plan was to modify the weather by seeding the cloud formations, thus making rain clouds produce more moisture than they might under normal conditions.

"We were careful not to make claims that the machines had made it rain," Cox recalled.

Krick's rainmaking plan called for silver iodide to be sent aloft mixed with hot air generated by a small furnace "like one in a blacksmith shop," Cox explained. First the furnace was fired with charcoal, later with coke impregnated with silver iodide. Fumes would rise straight up, Cox said, then the chemicals would spread out in the light air.

Cox described his rainmaking machine, or furnace, as real small. He kept it behind his service station and would fire it up when the Denver office called him to notify him that conditions were right.

"We stayed in touch by telephone," Cox said. A part of his job was to notify the Denver office daily about cloud formations, wind direction, wind velocity, and other conditions.

The Krick project covered an area from Brady, in the central part of Texas, to San Antonio and then back to Waco, and the Denver scientist had similar rainmaking generators in Kerrville, Llano, Sterling City, Ballinger, Lamesa, and Big Spring.

"By seeding the clouds passing over our area, rains would be generated by the time those same clouds got over Fredericksburg and San Antonio," Cox said.

Ironically, Krick also warned his rainmaking machine generator operators when not to turn on the apparatus.

Cox said Krick's office told him not to turn on the machine on the day that violent thunderstorms kicked off tornadoes that struck the Lake View section of San Angelo and downtown Waco.

"He told us not to turn on the machine when that cloud formation came over. He said it was a dangerous cloud, and he didn't want us to mess with it," Cox continued.

Krick's rainmaking program was utilized in a number of Texas locations during the 1950s where he received contracts to work around Dallas, Midland, San Antonio, Waco, and other communities. Efforts were made to generate enough money by San Angelo area residents to start a rainmaking program, but only a small amount was collected. Most of the monies came from voluntary assessments of a penny or more per acre of land. The Krick organization proposed that the seven-county area around San Angelo, composed of some 15.3 million acres, would cost a flat payment of $60,000 plus a performance payment of up to $120,000.

Cox said he was paid about $1 per hour to maintain and operate the rainmaking generator at his service station. The Krick organization furnished all the chemicals, and when the project was completed, the firm picked up the machine.

Rainmaking is nothing new in arid West Texas. In 1910 folks living in the Carlsbad-Water Valley area north of San Angelo were fascinated by three tower-like structures set up by a man named Charles Hatfield.

Hatfield's towers were actually rainmaking laboratories on stilts. From these twenty-five-foot-tall towers, Hatfield would pump various chemicals into the air. His theory was the chemicals would form clouds, and to speed up the process he would later send up balloons loaded with two sticks of dynamite.

In time some rain did fall, and Hatfield took credit for the showers. However, folks living in the area were not impressed, claiming that it would have rained anyway.

About six years later, Hatfield was in California where he agreed to produce enough rain to fill San Diego's Morena Reservoir, which had dried up because of extreme drought, if the city council would pay him $10,000. Four days after he had set up his twenty-five-foot-tall towers on the banks of the reservoir it started to rain —and rain—and rain. The reservoir overflowed, washing out 109 bridges in San Diego County. The roads were so muddy that Hatfield could not get to town on horseback. Members of the city council, faced with all kinds of threats from a mad citizenry, refused to pay him, saying it would have rained anyhow.

Another prominent rainmaker was C. W. Post, the cereal king, who bought some 200,000 acres of land in Garza and Lynn Counties and had a Texas Panhandle town named for him. When Post needed rain during the same 1910 drought that brought Hatfield to the Carlsbad-Water Valley area, he believed he could make it rain by exploding massive amounts of dynamite.

Post, a military history student, noted that nearly every description of battle where heavy artillery was used mentioned rain falling in sometimes massive amounts.

Post staged some eighteen "rain battles" over several dry years, but records show that only three rains of any significance came after the explosions ceased. Only the Dupont Powder Company realized any profit from the rain battles. The explosive manufacturer had agreed to share the expense of a part of the experiment.

Rainmaking experiments also were conducted at Midland in 1891 when General Robert St. George Dyrenforth used explosive balloons and artillery shells to "break the balanced state" of nature and make rain clouds develop. This experiment was conducted by the U.S. Department of Agriculture and funded by Congress. The experiment was inconclusive and was ended after only one season.

Robert J. Kleberg, operator of the giant King Ranch in South Texas, employed the same group of experimenters to try and make it rain on the ranch. Although some heavy rain occurred, few responsible scientists were willing to attribute the rainfall to the explosives.

A number of years went by until Krick and several other so-called "experts" attempted different weather modification programs. Although Krick's projects were mostly inconclusive, his pioneering efforts paved the way for modern seeding attempts using dry ice and other chemicals.

The number of commercial weather-modification projects increased markedly in Texas in the 1950s and 1960s, which prompted the State Legislature to adopt a statute controlling cloud-seeding operations. The Texas Weather Modification Act of 1967 charged the Texas Water Development Board to license and permit weather modification work in the state and to promote research and development in weather-modification technology. The act is now a part of the Texas Water Code.

Since passage of the act, there have been a number of projects conducted to stimulate rainfall. Programs designed to increase rainfall have been sponsored by the Colorado River Municipal Water District in Big Spring, the Edwards Underground Water District in San Antonio, the city of San Angelo, and the city of Corpus Christi. With one exception, the projects were not conducted long enough to allow proper evaluation. The exception is the CRMWD's program, which has indicated that the program has resulted in increased precipitation in the target area.

Humpy Jackson Fought Army Three Years

The Menard Frontiersman Gave 4th Cavalrymen Bad Time

A LOVE NOTE from an army cavalryman to a young schoolgirl stirred up the Menardville community, created havoc for troopers stationed at Fort McKavett, and put her frontiersman-father on the run for about three years. Several people were to die because of the situation, and others were to suffer the long-term effects of imprisonment.

John Monroe Jackson, better known as "Humpy" Jackson because of the hump on his broad shoulders, came to Menard County before the Civil War when it was raw frontier land. During the Civil War when there were no military units to protect the settlers, Jackson served as a scout for the local militia, thus he knew the headwaters of the San Saba River like the wrinkles in his hand.

Humpy Jackson is well remembered by folks living in the Menard area of Central Texas. He was a colorful and unusual man, because not only was he a pioneer settler of Menardville, he also kept the countryside stirred up for some three years while elements of the U.S. Cavalry chased him for murder.

Frontier historian-newspaperman J. Marvin Hunter knew Humpy Jackson during those times and did several stories about Jackson's killing of a soldier named "Lanky Jim," who allegedly had written a love note

Right: *Humpy Jackson, frontiersman-outlaw. Photo courtesy* Menard News.

to one of Jackson's daughers, Narcissa, fourteen. The soldier, a light-skinned black man, was among a group of soldiers working at a sawmill near the Jackson farm on the San Saba River. He had seen the girl walking home from school and took a fancy to her.

"Yes, it is generally believed in the family that Narcissa was the one who got the note," said Barbara Chapman Elliott of San Angelo, one of Humpy's great-great-great-grandchildren. Some early stories about the incident did not reveal the daughter's name.

According to Hunter's version and that of Menard historian N. H. Pierce, Humpy Jackson was furious when he learned that one of the soldiers had written such a note to his girl. Whether Jackson went immediately to find the soldier or waited until the next day is unclear. However, he did wait in ambush and shoot one of the soldiers on the sawmill detail with deadly accuracy, hitting the man in the head and killing him instantly.

The rash act brought tremendous hardship to the Jackson family, who saw their home burned and their livestock taken as a result of Humpy's fleeing the army search parties. Humpy

Jackson, an experienced and seasoned frontiersman, knew how to live in the woods and eventually eluded the soldiers as well as Lieutenant John Bullis's Seminole Indian scouts for about three years. Colonel Ranald S. Mackenzie, then commander of the 4th Cavalry Regiment, was furious that his experienced troopers could not find and capture the elusive Jackson.

One day while traveling by horseback near the Peg Leg Stage Station located about twelve miles east of Menardville, Jackson was spotted by a cavalry patrol. Ironically, most of the black soldiers stationed at Fort McKavett did not know what Jackson looked like; particularly they did not know of the prominent hump on his back. If Jackson had played his cards right that day when he encountered the patrol, the soldiers perhaps would have let him pass undetected.

Rather than remain in the open, Jackson spurred his horse into a mesquite flat that was thick with various sizes of trees. Riding one horse and leading another into the trees, Jackson accidentally let the horse being led by a rope go on one side of a tree while his mount

Colonel Ranald Mackenzie, 4th Cavalry Commander. Photo courtesy Fort Concho National Historic Site, San Angelo.

went on the other. He was pulled from the saddle and slammed to the ground. When the soldiers reached the fallen man, he moaned loudly and complained that he had broken his back and asked the soldiers to take him home. Seeing the huge swelling between his shoulders, the troopers quickly helped to aid the man the best they could, and four of the troopers said they would take him home on a horse-drawn stretcher made of tree limbs and blankets. The patrol did not believe the man would live very long in his injured condition.

While several of the soldiers

went to Fort McKavett to report Jackson's capture, four others took him home and set up a guard detail about the house.

A man named Billy Epps, who had been hired to help the Jackson family look after the family farm, went to Menardville and reported that Jackson had been captured and was being held at his home by soldiers. Quickly, friends of Jackson gathered to figure out a way to rescue him. Several men were chosen to carry out the plan, including George Harvey, Pete Crane, Steve Caveness, and Charley Owens.

When Humpy Jackson was brought into his home by the soldiers, his other daughter, Henrietta Elizabeth, assisted the men in putting her father into bed. She also slipped her father a pistol, which quickly went beneath the bedcovers.

When the rescuers rushed the soldiers standing guard in the yard and fired their weapons, Jackson pulled his pistol from beneath the heavy quilt and shot the soldier guarding him in the house. Two other soldiers were killed in the gunfight outside, but the third soldier fell and rolled toward the river. When the four friends went into Jackson's house, the wounded soldier who had rolled into the river struggled out of the water and walked most of the way to Fort McKavett, more than twenty-five miles away, before finding a horse to ride in order to give the alarm. Meanwhile, Jackson quickly dressed, gathered some food supplies, and mounted a horse and fled to the hills.

Although Jackson made his escape, three of his rescuers fared badly. Crane was eventually killed in Pecos by a deputy sheriff. Caveness never made it out of the county. He was overtaken by soldiers and killed. Owens also was killed a short time later in Llano County. Only Harvey escaped.

The Jackson family was arrested and jailed at Fort McKavett. Their home, barn, and crops were burned and livestock were killed by order of the fort commander. Many Menard residents were arrested and questioned concerning the escape plot and the killing of the soldiers. When the soldiers came to destroy the Jackson homestead, they also arrested Mrs. Jackson and her children and placed them in the guardhouse where they remained for several days.

Several prominent Menardville citizens went to the fort to plead for their release. They were finally permitted to return to their burned-out home. The family was able to survive because neighbors brought them food, provided some furniture, and helped rebuild their house.

Humpy Jackson was a hunted man for nearly two more years. He was given food by friends and others living in the countryside, but he lived in several caves along the San Saba River in order that none of his friends or neighbors would be accused of providing him with lodging. Ultimately, the search for Humpy Jackson was ended by the soldiers when the county was officially recognized and civil authorities took over.

When the district court was convened in the new county, Humpy Jackson's case was the first ever investigated by the grand jury, but the grand jury refused to indict him for the killing of the soldiers so he was a free man. By this time Fort McKavett had been declared surplus property, and soldiers were moved elsewhere.

But Humpy Jackson's life was destroyed. His health was fast failing, and his wife, Elizabeth, had chosen to separate from him and go live with a daughter. He died in 1890 and was buried in Menard's Pioneer Rest Cemetery. Elizabeth died on February 27, 1905, and was buried by her husband, despite spending most of their final years separated.

Part II

Places

Remnants of the Past

FROM CONCHO TO WELFARE, and from Juno to Fort Griffin, there are plenty of ghost towns for Texans to visit. Some were once importance stops on the state's route to progress. Others, like Texon and Best, were created and died in less than a half century.

The state's official travel guide only lists nine ghost towns. The *Roads of Texas* says there are at least 100 ghost towns in the state, and veteran historian Ed Bartholomew says there are more than 800.

I believe a town reaches the level of ghost town when it loses its post office. As such, the famous ghost town of Terlingua in the Texas Big Bend country is still alive. It has a post office, although it is located more than a mile down the road from the picturesque piles of stone that once housed hundreds of mine workers.

My interest in ghost towns grew as a result of an inquiry from a friend of my wife, Jean. She asked if I had ever been to Welfare, the almost forgotten community between Comfort and Boerne, and how had that place gotten its unusual name.

Welfare, located four miles southeast of Waring in west central Kendall County, was once called Bon Ton, or Boyton, apparently using the name of an early-day settler. However, when the post office was established in 1880, the name became Welfare, possibly for the German word *wohifarht,* meaning pleasant trip.

In 1887 the San Antonio and Aransas Pass Railway Company finished a section of track between San Antonio and Kerrville, which provided Welfare an easy access to markets for its agricultural products. In 1892 the community had 275 residents, and the school there had 20 pupils. The school continued to operate until 1952 when it consolidated with Comfort schools.

Much of Welfare's history revolves around transportation routes and the railroad, according to my friend Garland Perry, who wrote a history of Kendall County several years ago. Perry says mail was first delivered to Welfare by bicycle, then by stagecoach on a twice-a-week

Above: *Cleo store long abandoned, with new mailboxes. Ross McSwain collection.*

basis. Later the railroad brought in the mail. At one time the town had a depot and water tank, saloon, hotel, and cotton gin. As a result of drought, a major fire, and boll weevil infestation that made growing cotton more difficult, the town's population dwindled to twenty-five people. When U.S. Highway 87 bypassed the community in 1930, and when the railroad ceased to run, Welfare's death knell started to ring. The post office closed in 1976. An old store building was the only commercial structure still in existence when I last traveled to Welfare. Perry says the old store was constructed in 1890 and that a man named

Percy Laas worked in the post office and store for fifty-five years. It's hard to find that kind of devoted employee in today's job market.

Most of Texas's ghost towns of record have few residents. Some have been completely abandoned, while others are still holding on, perhaps as a tourist attraction.

Some writers have included Mentone and Langtry in their lists of ghost towns, but these communities have folks residing there and have businesses. Others that have some people residing in the community or nearby are Stiles in Reagan County, Sherwood in Irion County, Luckenbach in Gillespie County, and Thurber in Erath County.

Thurber has an interesting history. Once the largest town between Fort Worth and El Paso, Thurber was founded in the 1880s by the Johnson Coal Company. When the firm was unable to meet its payroll, the miners called a strike and the mines were closed. In 1888 the mines were sold to the Texas and Pacific Coal Company. The company named the mining camp "Thurber" and owned everything in the town—from the coal mines below the surface to the opera house. It was the first completely electrified town in the Southwest. Despite improvements, the company was still saddled with miners' strikes and the threat of strikes. In 1903 another strike was called when the miners attempted to organize a union. When it was settled, Thurber became the only 100 percent union in the world.

During its heyday, Thurber's opera house drew some of the country's foremost entertainers.

When oil was discovered in nearby Ranger in 1917, competi-tion from the petroleum industry made it difficult to sell coal to the railroads. When the Texas and Pacific Coal and Oil Company attempted to operate its mines with nonunion workers, it was forced to close down. The town was eventually ordered abandoned in 1933.

In another time, many of these old towns bustled with all kinds of activity. What happened to them? Why are they no longer thriving?

Most of the ghost towns in Texas died because something happened to cause them to no longer be needed. Perhaps the railroad bypassed them. In another case a hurricane wiped the town off the map, and the Texas coastline. This happened to the port of Indianola, which at one time was larger than the port of Galveston.

In order to visit some of these ghost towns, a traveler must get off the main roads. Langtry, once a thriving railroad town, is off the beaten path along U.S. Highway 90 between Del Rio and Sanderson. Although there are still some families living in the town and in the vicinity, the only commercial operation is a gift shop across from the Judge Roy Bean Visitor

Center, operated by the Texas Department of Transportation. Persons needing a loaf of bread must travel more than thirty miles to Comstock.

Helena, a community in Karnes County southeast of San Antonio, is said to have died because of one gunfight too many. Emmett Butler, twenty, son of the area's wealthiest rancher, was shot to death in a saloon in 1884. When the distraught father was unable to determine who killed his son, he vowed to kill the town. He did so by donating land to the railroad miles away from the town when the railroad builders came across South Texas.

The railroad also bypassed Harmony Hill in Rusk County near Marshall. When first established in 1850, it was called Nip and Tuck. A storm destroyed the town in 1906, leaving behind a large cemetery.

Fort Phantom Hill, located in Jones County north of Abilene, was never a real town, but it was a frontier post for the Army prior to the Civil War. It was established in 1851 and later burned by the Indians when troops vacated the fort because of a shortage of water. Its many tall chimneys and a rock powder house remain. The village

of Phantom Hill, located nearby, sprouted up as settlers came into Jones County. However, it was soon abandoned when it lost out to Anson as the county seat.

Rath City, located near Hamlin, was a thriving trading post for less than two years. It was the center of trading for buffalo hunters and hide traders. When the buffalo were killed out, the trading post operators moved on. Today, all that remains of Rath City is a historical marker and several graves located in the middle of a wheat field.

There are two ghost towns in Coke County: Sanco and Silver. Sanco is the typical West Texas ghost town with its long abandoned general store, a church last used for a funeral, a crumbling schoolhouse, and a tabernacle. It was a ranch community. Silver, located north of Sanco, was an agricultural community until Sun Oil Company discovered oil in Coke County in 1946. The oil boom brought in nearly 1,000 new residents who lived in oil company camps or housing. When oil production began to decrease, people started leaving for other locations. Silver's once high-dollar school building is now used for a barn.

Belle Plain, which served as the

first Callahan County seat, later lost out to Baird when the Texas and Pacific Railroad bypassed the town in 1881. At its peak, Belle Plain had more than 400 families living there. Thirteen years after the railroad bypassed the town, there were only two families still calling the place home.

Some folks traveling to Ivie Reservoir pass the ghost town of Concho, located on Farm to Market Road 1929. Concho was founded about 1910, and by 1920 there were twenty persons living in the community. When Concho was abandoned after World War II, there were only two businesses and a post office remaining. Today, a picturesque filling station remains at the site that is now private property.

Below: *Old Concho store and antique gas pump, now on private property. Photo courtesy* San Angelo Standard-Times.

Fort Chadbourne

The Indians Won the Horse Races

LIFE ON THE TEXAS FRONTIER for soldiers and settlers alike could be uncomfortable, dangerous, life threatening, and even hilarious, depending on the time of year and whether the soldiers, Indians, and settlers were getting along. This isolated fort, located about twelve miles north of Bronte on the Coke-Runnels County line, saw it all during its short life.

For many years the ruins of Fort Chadbourne were closed to the public. However, rancher Garland Richards and his wife, Lana, have now unlocked the gates to tourists and are working to stabilize the ruins and to save and catalog its many artifacts.

When Captain Daniel Whiting, an army surveyor, passed through Central Texas in 1849, he recommended that a fort be placed in the general vicinity of where Fort Chadbourne presently sits in quiet isolation on top of a hill overlooking Oak Creek.

Months went by before Whiting's recommendations were acted upon. On December 16, 1851, General Persifor F. Smith, commander of the 8th Military District in San Antonio, issued General Order No. 95, which established several new forts, including Fort Chadbourne.

The fort was located nearly in the center of Indian Territory, populated by some 20,000 Indians, including Comanches, Apaches, Kiowas, and other tribes. Many of the Indians lived in the near vicinity and traveled the area during the 1850s because the Colorado River Valley provided a vast grazing area for wildlife, particularly buffalo. As a result, there were conflicts between the Indians and the frontier explorers, settlers, and soldiers, including a brief but violent skirmish within the fort proper in 1856.

Because of its remote location, the fort offered little comfort to the soldiers. It was even worse for members of the soldiers' families.

When post surgeon Dr. Ebenezer Swift arrived with his wife, she quickly realized there was danger lurking everywhere from hostile Indians, rattlesnakes, roaming buffalo, and even the weather. Dr. Swift and post commander Captain Calhoun told Army Paymaster Colonel Albert Sidney Johnston in 1854 that a terrible hailstorm had struck the fort on June 9. The stones were so thick that there were drifts up to eight feet deep. Later that same year a swarm of hungry grasshoppers passed through the area for three days. Soldiers reported that every plant was devoid of leaves, and forage was at a premium.

Another dangerous incident occurred that nearly cost the life of a soldier and a four-year-old girl. One day the fort inhabitants saw a huge dust cloud developing in the distance. It did not alarm folks at first because they were used to seeing blowing dust during dry times. However, when they started hearing a low rumbling noise, they realized it was a stampeding herd of buffalo. People dashed for cover as the thundering herd started to sweep toward the fort parade grounds. Everyone but the little girl made it to safety. When the soldier saw the child, he rushed to her rescue, putting her on his shoulders while he hugged a nearby tree as tight as he could.

> Dr. Swift and post commander Captain Calhoun told Army Paymaster Colonel Albert Sidney Johnston in 1854 that a terrible hailstorm had struck the fort on June 9. The stones were so thick that there were drifts up to eight feet deep.

After a few minutes passed, the inhabitants came outside to find the trooper and the little girl still hugging the tree, but covered in dust.

During those early years, the Indians were generally peaceful, but from time to time bands would go on raiding parties to steal horses and mules. The Butterfield stage line passed through Fort Chadbourne, thus the stage company's herds of animals were always a ready target for the Indians.

Both soldiers and settlers were in contact with the Indians on a regular basis. Both friendly and hostile Indians often camped at the fort's perimeter, carefully watched by the soldiers who had learned that certain Comanche chiefs were not trustworthy. As a result of certain incidents that occurred at the fort, the soldiers and civilians living in its vicinity tended to stay close to the fort grounds, especially after dark.

One September night, a soldier named Mattock made a visit to a

Above: *Ruins of Fort Chadbourne barracks. Ross McSwain collection.*

nearby saloon located just across Oak Creek. The saloon was run by a civilian trader. It was one of the few diversions that the soldiers had to escape the boredom.

As Mattock returned to the fort from the saloon by a narrow footbridge across Oak Creek, he was ambushed by six Comanches who shot him with fourteen arrows. Miraculously, Mattock was able to reach the fort where he was treated by Dr. Swift.

The fort surgeon noted in his journal that the soldier looked like a porcupine with all the arrows protruding from his body. Three of the arrows had penetrated Mattock's body so deeply that the

doctor had to extract them by cutting off the feathered part and pulling the shaft through the man's body. Although seriously wounded, Mattock survived and eventually completely recovered from his wounds. The only lasting effect was a limp that resulted from a lacerated nerve.

Friendly Indians, camped outside the fort perimeter, would beg for food. Cynthia Ann Parker, mother of Comanche war chief Quanah Parker, is said to have come to the fort often to beg for food. She would wear a bonnet to cover her light hair. She had been captured by Indians when she was nine years old and later was to become the wife of Chief Peta Nocona. She had two sons, Pecos and Quanah. In 1860, at the Battle of Peace River, Cynthia Ann and her two-year-old daughter, Prairie Flower, were captured. She was thirty-four years old. Taken to Fort Cooper, she was later recognized by her uncle Isaac Parker and returned to her family. However, she grieved for her Indian family and died a short time after her daughter died in 1863.

According to fort records, the Indian women and children who came to the fort often wore the clothes of captured white people, some of which still had visible bloodstains.

In July 1854 a serious incident occurred at the fort when Indians killed Captain Michael E. Van Buren. The following year, two soldiers carrying the mail were captured, tied to a tree, and then burned alive.

Major Seth Eastman rounded up several suspects in the atrocity. The Indians denied having taken part in the killing of the mail carriers, but Eastman recognized a gun one Indian was carrying as belonging to one of the dead troopers.

When the soldiers attempted to arrest the Indians, a fight broke out. Nine Indians were shot, but one of the chiefs managed to break away with a rifle and pistol and barricade himself inside Major Eastman's house at the edge of the parade ground. When the Indian refused to surrender, Lieutenant C. W. Thomas of the 1st Infantry ordered his men to break down the door. The officer ran into the room, and as the chief attempted to fire, Thomas shot him through the head.

Not all contact with the Indians was unfriendly. The Indians and the soldiers loved horse racing, and they would gamble heavily on the winners. One such event ended up as a humiliating lesson to the fort's officers.

Many of the fort's officers came from the East, and they took pride in owning fine thoroughbred horses. One young officer bragged that his fine horse could outrun any horse in Texas. One day a band of Indians came into the fort and challenged the officer to a race. He refused at first but eventually agreed to race when he was chided by fellow officers. The officers and Indians placed heavy bets on the race.

The Indian pony that the Comanches brought for the race was a wild mustang, about fourteen hands high, thin, and very shaggy in appearance. The animal looked nothing like a winner. In fact, it appeared that the horse had a better chance of winning if it was carried by the rider, a big, husky Indian weighing 150 pounds or more. Once the race started, the Indian used a war club to coax the pony to run. It beat the officer's long-legged thoroughbred by a neck.

The soldiers were bitter losers. Hoping to win back their wagers, they challenged the Indian to another race against another officer's thoroughbred horse. The Indian chief, Malaquetop, did not want to allow the race but finally gave in. The second race was much like the first—the Indian pony outran the officer's horse by a length.

After the second race, the troopers were getting upset over losing their wagers to the pitiful-looking horse. A third challenge was made to the Indians, and this time the soldiers entered a Kentucky thoroughbred mare. The Indians readily accepted and piled all kinds of goods on the blanket that served as a wager pile. The wager pot grew even bigger when the soldiers added their money and trading goods. The Kentucky mare was the fastest animal at the fort, having beaten every other horse in previous races by at least forty yards.

When the race started, it immediately became clear to the soldiers that the Indian pony was something special. The Indian brave astride the pony had thrown away his war club, bent low over the pony's back, and shrieked loudly into the pony's ear. The mustang leaped forward and soon left the Kentucky mare far behind. During the last fifty yards of the quarter-mile race, the Indian turned around backwards on his mount, shouted obscenities at the soldiers, and made vulgar gestures at the soldier riding the thoroughbred.

When the Comanches left, carrying away a blanket loaded with valuables, the soldiers learned from an interpreter that they had been victims of a cruel joke. The mustang was the fastest Indian pony on the plains. The Indians had already pulled the same prank on a Kickapoo tribe, winning more than 600 horses through wagers on the pony.

Fort Chadbourne was one of the principal Texas frontier forts prior to the Civil War. In March 1854 Comanches came from all directions to the fort to sign a treaty agreeing to settle on a reservation near Fort Belknap. According to Floyd J. Holmes, who compiled the Indian Papers in Texas and the Southwest, an estimated 26,000 men, women, and children camped around the fort at various times before moving onto the reservation.

Artifacts from the fort's active period fill shelves and cabinets at rancher Garland Richards' office, located on the old fort grounds. The fort became private property in 1876 when the late Thomas L. Odom and his son, Garland G. Odom, drove 4,000 head of cattle from their ranch near San Antonio and established the O.D. Ranch. Odom used the fort as headquarters for his cattle operations that eventually encompassed more than 100,000 acres of land in Coke, Runnels, and Nolan Counties. The Odoms used the fort buildings until they were replaced by more substantial structures. As the fort buildings were phased out of use, they were not maintained, thus over the years the fort structures decayed. Today, some of the walls of barracks still stand while others have disappeared.

Now, Thomas Odom's great-great-grandson, Garland Richards, is working to preserve the integrity of the fort and stabilize the remaining structures. In January 1999 Richards and his wife, Lana, created the Fort Chadbourne Foundation for the purpose of protecting and preserving the historic site and its heritage and to promote the fort's social and cultural significance.

"My grandfather's insistence in keeping the ranch closed to the public actually made the place safe from artifact hunters," Richards said. The site has untold numbers of archeological locations that have produced scores of artifacts dating to both Indian and soldier periods.

"This is a special place. It is unique. I want the youngsters to get to know more about the history of the area. Young people today don't seem to appreciate history. I want to change that," Richards said.

Old Fort Chadbourne contains about twenty-five acres and is located nearly in the center of Garland Richards' portion of the Fort Chadbourne Ranch. The fort property is now open during daylight hours for self-guided tours. For information, contact the Fort Chadbourne Foundation, 651 U.S. Highway 277, Bronte, Texas 76933, or call (915) 743-2555. There is no admission fee, but donations are accepted and appreciated.

Brambletye

THE UNUSUAL-LOOKING THREE-STORY HOUSE that sits prominently on a hill overlooking Bear Creek in northwest Kimble County is a rare example of late nineteenth-century English vernacular architecture in the Texas Hill Country. Some people say the place has ghosts; others say a mysterious light glows from the third story at certain times of the year.

Folks who have lived in the immediate area of the house just shug their shoulders about the ghosts, although some "ghostly" things have occured at Brambletye in years past.

According to Frederica Wyatt of Junction, Kimble County's most knowledgeable historian, Brambletye was constructed between 1895 and 1900 by an English immigrant, William Hall, who came to Texas in 1888. Hall, an eccentric gentleman, built his Texas castle but did not live long enough to see it completed. Ironically, the house had a hand in causing Hall's untimely death. While working on a gateway at the house, Hall cut himself. He developed blood poisoning from the wound and was taken to San Antonio for medical care. He died there on March 30, 1900.

In a memoir titled *I Remember,* William Hall's son, Fred, and another man, Hudson Stuck, had discussed leaving England for either Australia or America. They flipped a coin to make the decision. Stuck and Fred Hall arrived in San Antonio in 1885.

Stuck, who taught at the Bear Creek School for a time, later became an archdeacon in the Episcopal church and led the first expedition of climbers that successfully scaled the south peak of Mount McKinley in Alaska.

William Hall followed his son to Texas in 1888 in the company of a man named E. E. "Ted" Bolt. Hall lived on the Bolt ranch before he constructed Brambletye. The Bolt ranch was in the same vicinity as the Brambletye place, a few miles southeast. Hall had purchased the land on Bear Creek in 1895 for $460.

According to historian Wyatt, the ghost legends that have shrouded Brambletye for more than a century came about when one of Hall's daughters, Mae,

married Manuel Morales in 1892.

"It was certainly not conventional (in those early days) for an Anglo to marry into a Hispanic family, and stories have circulated and recirculated about the event," Mrs. Wyatt notes. One story was told that Mae was locked upstairs until she finally consented to marry Manuel, but that was untrue. "The house was not even built at the time of the marriage," Wyatt added. "In fact, William Hall did not even own the ranch at the time of the marriage."

Another story, also untrue, relates that a beautiful young woman was found hanging from a rope looped over an upper rafter at Brambletye, apparently having chosen suicide rather than to live without her lover.

Wyatt says that one writer penned, "Every castle must have a ghost, even a junior grade castle. There must be lights in an upper window and screams. So Brambletye got its ghost. At least two. Their names: Gossip and Prejudice. They may still be around."

Mae Hall married into a well-respected family. Manuel Morales was the son of Meliton and Ramona Morales, who came from South Texas to settle on Bear Creek, then called Viejo Creek, in 1874. The Morales family brought 2,000 sheep, 200 head of Spanish goats, a herd of horses, and two dogs with them when they settled on their ranch located near a freight route that connected San Antonio with Fort McKavett and Fort Concho, where present-day San Angelo is located.

Brambletye has been owned by several different families. Today the historic ranch and home is owned by an Austin man, James R. George Jr.

Not only is Brambletye a Texas historical landmark, it also is included on the National Register of Historic Places.

Brambletye is not open to the public, however, it can be seen from Farm to Market Road 2291, that runs from Interstate 10 north to the community of Cleo and to Menard.

eft: *Brambletye, an Englishman's Texas* ıstle. *Ross McSwain collection.*

The Indians Won Some, Too

Peaceful Kickapoos Whip the Texas Militia

CONFEDERATE SOLDIERS AND TEXAS MILITIA got a decisive country whipping in a fight with a bunch of peaceful Kickapoo Indians near the town of Mertzon in Irion County nearly 140 years ago. It was the only battle ever fought by Confederate troops in the Central Texas area.

It was a bleak, cold, and snowy January 8, 1865, when the state troops working the frontier decided to "take a whack at a beehive with a short stick," stirring up some 2,000 Kickapoo Indians who had made camp on Dove Creek about eight miles east of Mertzon on what is best known as the Winterbotham ranch. The Indians were traveling to Mexico from Oklahoma where they had lived fairly peacefully along the Canadian River.

The Kickapoos were a tribe of English-speaking Indians who had been friendly to the white man until buffalo hunters invaded their hunting ground and farmers came in and took over their croplands in Kansas. It was just easier to move on to new territory than attempt to live close to the intruders, thus the first bunch of Kickapoos went to Mexico with their chief, Wildcat. Others settled on the Canadian River in western Oklahoma.

The Kickapoos were not friendly to the South, either, so Mexico was the safest place to relocate. It was during this mass exodus south that the Dove Creek battle occurred, and few people to this day understand why such a fight happened.

The late Leta Crawford, longtime Irion County historian, spent decades gathering information on the battle. She was the daughter of Fayette Tankersley and a granddaughter of R. F. Tankersley, one of the first cowmen to settle in the Mertzon area.

Fayette Tankersley was six years old when the battle occurred, and he rode in a wagon with his father to the battlefield to help bury the dead. Some two-dozen men lost their lives that cold January day. Other records say that more than thirty men were killed in the fight.

With the beginning of the Civil War, both the Union and the Confederacy sought the aid of various Indian tribes. As a result of this

Above: *Kickapoo Indians look at Dove Creek Battlefield marker.*

and attempting to avoid any involvement in the white man's war, the Kickapoos set out through Texas in their journey to Mexico. Their effort to remain neutral ended when the three Kickapoo bands, camping on Dove Creek near the ranch headquarters of R. F. Tankersley, were attacked by the Confederate cavalry and Texas militiamen. Although surprised and outgunned, the Indians repelled their attackers.

Some history resources say there were about 1,400 Kickapoos in the encampment. The state troops, composed of Confederate cavalry, militiamen, and some Texas Rangers, totaled about 370 men. They were commanded by Captain Henry Fossett.

Historian William C. Pool, who prepared an article for the *Southwestern Historical Quarterly,* notes that the Indians were led by Chief No-Ko-Wat.

In a desperate battle, the Texans were soundly defeated, Pool notes. The state troops lost 36 men killed and 60 wounded. Indian losses were much less, with 11 reported killed and 31 wounded. However, historical markers at the battlefield and at Mertzon tell a different story, noting that 22 Texans were killed and 18 were wounded. Indian losses were never really known since by custom, Indians always removed their dead from a battlefield if at all possible.

What was the reason for the fight? Some say it was over some horses that had been stolen from the R. F. Tankersley ranch. However, Tankersley reports that Kickapoos helped to return his horses because he allowed them to camp and rest on his ranch during their journey to Mexico.

Apparently the battle came about after a scouting party of state troops commanded by Captain N. W. Gillentine had traced the Kickapoo trail and reported the Indians on the move to Lieutenant Colonel James Barry at Fort Belknap.

Constantly aware of possible Indian trouble on the frontier, Barry sounded the alarm, and

word reached Stephenville, then headquarters of the Texas Militia assigned to Frontier District 2. Captain S. S. Totten, second in command, immediately rallied his troops and headed for western Texas where he joined up with

Captain John Fossett's detachment of Confederates.

The bloody battle along the west side of Dove Creek lasted about five hours. As a result of the fight, the once peaceful Kickapoos

Left: *Grave marker for one of the militia killed at Dove Creek battle.* Below: *Lonely battlefield now on private property. Photos courtesy* San Angelo Standard-Times.

would later use the fight as an excuse to raid Anglo settlers along the U.S.-Mexico border.

What has puzzled most historians about the Dove Creek battle is the reason for it. From what R. F. Tankersley relates about the horse

incident, the Indians were minding their manners and trying to stay out of trouble. Their movement away from the settlements and to the far reaches of the frontier in trying to reach their Mexico destination also backs up this theory.

Obviously, lots of mistakes were made. There was no "council of war," and the Anglo forces apparently made no effort to learn why the Indians were in the area. Also, the state troops apparently assumed that the Indians were hostile, and they planned the attack without knowing even to what tribe the Indians belonged. What really cut the cake was the death of the Indian chief and a young woman, possibly his daughter, who came to parley with the leaders of the militia under a white flag.

An investigation by Brigadier General J. D. McAdoo cited the Anglo commanders for failing to hold a council of war, complacency to provide orders to the various units, failure to form a line of battle, and failing to learn what tribe they were dealing with prior to charging the camp.

After the Kickapoos reached Mexico, they teamed up with other more hostile Indians in raiding settlements along the Rio Grande, using the Dove Creek battle as an excuse for their depredations.

By the early 1870s Kickapoo raids had become a serious problem. Many Texans called on the cavalry to stop the raiding, even suggesting that the cavalry violate the international border and subdue the offenders.

On May 18, 1873, Colonel Ranald S. Mackenzie's 4th U.S. Cavalry, under orders from General Phillip H. Sheridan, did just that. Mackenzie planned his attack to coincide with a major Kickapoo hunt. The cavalry, some 400-men strong, attacked the Kickapoo camp near Remolino while most of the men were away on the hunt. After a brief skirmish, forty surviving Indians, mostly women, children, and those too old or sick to hunt, were captured and taken to San Antonio and later transferred to Fort Gibson in Indian Territory. These captives, held as hostages, resulted in many of the Kickapoos surrendering. More than 300 gave up and were removed to Indian Territory. However, most of the tribe refused to leave Mexico and gathered at El Nacimiento.

Today the Mexican Kickapoos are distinguished by their retention of traditional culture, ranging from religion to home construction to language and education; the Kickapoo way of life has survived, even if somewhat modified. Most of the Mexican Kickapoos, numbering about 625 people, spend the majority of their time in El Nacimiento, about 130 miles southwest of Eagle Pass. They are still semi-nomads.

The Dove Creek battlefield is on private property, behind fence and a locked gate. The battlefield marker, which contains the names of the commanders, keeps Totten and Fossett from gaining any more fame than what history has accorded them. Under the circumstance, that perhaps is justice.

The Mining Town That Fizzled Twice

ECONOMIC BOOMS AND BUSTS are nothing new to many West Texas communities, but there aren't too many towns around the state that have become a ghost town twice in the same century.

Shafter, once the richest place in Texas with more than 30 million ounces of silver produced from beneath its hardscrabble desert, has been a boomtown twice, but the silver strikes dwindled both times, and the picturesque little town on Cibolo Creek in southwest Presidio County has been deserted twice by its residents, leaving behind crumbling buildings and graves by the score in its lonely cemetery.

During the last census, Shafter had 26 residents, down tremendously from the early 1900s when Shafter was at its peak with some 3,000 persons, including a large number of Irish miners who had come to the area from California.

That may all change in the near future if silver prices rise. The huge silver mine that sits beneath the rolling hills was recently sold to Rio Grande Mining Company, operated by Robert Quartermain. Silver must bring at least $7 per ounce in order for it to be profitable to bring the mine back into operation. Previously, the property was held by Gold Fields Mining Corporation of New York, which started a feasibility study of reopening the mine in 1977. When Gold Fields shut down its operations at Shafter, the firm had spent more than $10 million drilling new shafts, digging and renovating more than 6,000 feet of tunnels, installing elevators, and putting into place a new head frame over the 1,000-foot-deep main shaft. For months Shafter experienced some new growth as miners and engineers came to the remote area to work. However, operations were suspended because the silver market suffered a very serious decline.

The new property holders, Rio Grande Mining, have told newspaper editor Robert Halpern of Marfa that the company plan calls for mining 2.5 million to 3 million ounces of silver a year over the life of the

project, about eight to ten years. Company officials believe there are 20 million ounces of silver in the ore vein proper and a total of 35 million ounces overall remaining in the mine.

According to Dr. Cecilia Thompson's book *History of Marfa and Presidio County*, Volume 1, the first commercial mining exploration was apparently carried out in southern Presidio County and the Chinati Mountains between January 16 and April 27, 1880. The venture was financed by the Galveston, Harrisburgh and San Antonio Railway Company. One of the local men involved was

Above: *Ruins of old Shafter mine ore processing plant. Photo courtesy* San Angelo Standard-Times.

early-day Presidio settler John Spencer.

Spencer, who worked a small silver mine in the area in the 1870s, apparently was asked to take part in the exploration because of his knowledge of the area. His small mine yielded high-grade ore, but he had to haul it by wagon to Chihuahua City, Mexico, to have it processed. The long haul, of about 160 miles, made the venture unprofitable.

According to early reports,

Above: *Old Shafter mine entry with
discarded timber bracing. Photo courtesy*
San Angelo Standard-Times.

Spencer probably knew the whereabouts of the silver deposits, but facts as to how he learned of them have long been overshadowed by more colorful stories. Some say Spencer took a sample of the ore to General William R. Shafter, then commander at Fort Davis, to find out if it was valuable. However, historian Thompson says it would have been illogical that an experienced miner like Spencer would need an army officer's opinion on such matters. She believes Spencer showed the general the ore sample to gain his interest so that Shafter would provide protection against the Indians.

According to records, Spencer shared his find with Shafter before October 12, 1880, when Alice Bullis, the wife of Lieutenant John L. Bullis, bought the land where the silver deposit was located. Alice Bullis bought the land because her husband had already taken up all the land he was entitled to under state law.

The Presidio Mining Company was later organized on October 20, 1883, and actual mining operations

Left top: *Weathered wooden crosses mark graves in Shafter graveyard.* Left bottom: *Ghost town of Shafter in Presidio County, Texas has come to life. Photos courtesy* San Angelo Standard-Times.

started in 1884 with a town springing up around the mine site. Later the Cibolo Creek Mill and Mining Company was organized in February 1884 to mill and process the ore. The mill and the mining company were consolidated in 1885.

The Presidio mine produced $300,000 worth of silver annually for a number of years and was one of the most consistent producers of silver in the country. From 1884 until it closed in 1942, it produced 2 million tons of ore from which 30,293,606 ounces of silver were made. This amount totaled nearly the entire output for the state.

The old Shafter mine reportedly covered an area of about nine square miles, and its underground workings included some seventy miles of tunnels, drifts, shafts, raises, and crosscuts. Historians say the mine was relatively safe with only three mine-related deaths reported from 1900 to its closing in 1942.

The town of Shafter, located near the mine entrance and named after General Shafter, developed as milling operations increased. A post office was established there in 1885. At its peak operation, the mine employed more than 300 men. Workers came from all over the country and included several ethnic groups. Mexican citizens and black Americans found better paying jobs working in the mines, and miners from California worked there as well until they left to prospect for Alaska gold in 1897.

Shafter miners lived in company-owned houses, shopped at the company store, and received medical care from the company doctor.

Some prospectors in the Trans-Pecos country believe that gold exists in the Shafter mine, and some of the precious metal has been found there but in limited amounts. According to the *Handbook of Texas*, most of the gold produced has come as a byproduct of silver and copper ores, but traces of gold have been found in the Shafter, Van Horn, Allanmoore, and the Quitman Mountains of West Texas.

Family's Abrupt Departure Leaves Mystery

Ostrander Ranch House Believed To Be Haunted

WHAT REALLY HAPPENED in the late 1880s to make the prominent Ostrander family vacate their palatial home?

For many years all kinds of speculation surrounded the family departure. Many believe the house to be haunted. Was a ghastly murder the reason for the abandonment? There were all kinds of tales of blood dripping down on the second floor from the third-floor belfry, leaving a stain that supposedly remains to this day.

Over the years curiosity has induced many people to drive hundreds of miles to see the mysterious landmark, located about twenty-five miles from San Angelo on the old Paint Rock Road.

The Ostrander house, a three-story structure of frame and native stone, is located on the once far-reaching Thornfield estate, named after an area that had a heavy growth of algerita brush. The house was built in the early 1880s of native limestone and heavy outer timbers that had been shipped by rail to Abilene then hauled by wagon to the

ranch. The interior was finished in imported Spanish oak.

The home's owner and builder, Weldon B. Ostrander, came to West Texas from New York with his half-brother, John A. Loomis. The men bought a 70,000-acre ranch, and built large homes on the ranch about twenty miles

> The Ostrander house, a three-story structure of frame and native stone, is located on the once far-reaching Thornfield estate, named after an area that had a heavy growth of algerita brush. The house was built in the

apart. Loomis called his part of the ranch Silver Cliff.

The late Dean Chenoweth, for many years the editor-in-chief of the *San Angelo Standard-Times* and recognized historian, recalled many years ago the story of the Loomis-Ostrander business relationship and their ranching operations, and he had the most likely answers to why the Ostanders left the home in "such a hurry" that food was left on the dining table, work clothes were left draped about the fine furniture, and the beds had not been correctly made up for the day.

Loomis was from a well-to-do Syracuse, New York, family, and he hankered for life in the West. He started scouting for land in Colorado, planning to set up his ranching headquarters at Trinidad. He had his eyes focused on ranchland in New Mexico, to be

early 1880s of native limestone and heavy outer timbers that had been shipped by rail to Abilene then hauled by wagon to the ranch. The interior was finished in imported Spanish oak.

bought in partnership with a man named John Townes. However, fate intervened when Frank and Dave McCarthy invited Loomis to join them on a trip to Texas.

Loomis was staying on the Mitchell Ranch on the Colorado River when a messenger came from the McCarthy Ranch saying that Tom McCarthy was in serious trouble—he had shot a Negro in San Angelo, and the Negro soldiers at Fort Concho had crossed

the Concho River into the fledgling community and shot up the town.

When the trial was called in Ben Ficklin, the Tom Green County site, Loomis was there along with the McCarthy brothers and other ranchers who went there to keep Tom from being lynched as the Negro soldiers had threatened.

All this activity was a dramatic introduction to the frontier for the young Easterner, who felt certain that the verdict of "accidental death" was correct. Tom McCarthy related to Loomis how he and some friends had tipped some musicians liberally while in a saloon, but when one of the musicians demanded more money, McCarthy had pulled his pistol and demanded that the man "beat it." The weapon went off when the man made a grab for it.

While getting Tom McCarthy out of town, Loomis and the others heard that the troopers were planning to avenge the black man's death by raiding the ranch and setting it on fire. When a traveler passed the ranch late one evening and asked to be allowed to spend the night, he was invited in. Later the men found the traveler's wagon loaded with army blankets.

Frank McCarthy alerted the others that night when he reported seeing a lantern swinging in the distance. As a result, Loomis, Frank, and the others dispersed into the brush and stayed there several hours before deciding that the rumors were false. The incident served to show Loomis how a fellow could get into trouble on the frontier without any fault of his own.

Loomis liked the country and chose to stay at Paint Rock to see if he could buy land. He met a land agent who directed him west to Lipan Creek where he started to buy acreage in the valley at prices from 50 cents to $1 per acre. This was the beginning of the Silver Cliff Ranch, which he was to operate until 1915.

Loomis' half-brother, Weldon Ostrander, became interested in West Texas and joined Loomis in 1885. It was against Loomis' better judgment that he entered into a partnership with Ostrander because the half-brother was obsessed with horses and the horse business. Loomis did not see any future in raising horses.

Ostrander went about building his house, which he called Thornfield, at a cost of $18,000, a very large sum in those days. However, he lived in the house only a few short years because his socialite wife had become bored with ranch life. They returned to Syracuse rather suddenly, but not like the legend says, "leaving behind food on the table." In addition, the Ostranders left their daughter behind to entertain her grandmother, who was living with them at the ranch.

Loomis also lived in the Ostrander house for about a year, but with the place vacant for more than thirty years, stories developed about a murder there. Red paint had run down on an inside wall, screech owls occupied the place, and some citizens said they had seen eerie lights in the house at night.

Loomis declared that the legend was merely that—a legend. He went about developing his own ranch, married in 1888, and his home, Silver Cliff, became the social center of the area.

At any rate, Ostrander returned to the ranch fifteen years later to sell the house furnishings at public auction. A Concho County settler bought much of the furniture, but it was destroyed in a fire in 1919.

Above: *Ostrander ranchhouse near Paint Rock, Texas. Photo courtesy* San Angleo Standard-Times.

In 1898 the ranch was sold to T. K. Wilson, who preferred to stay in the ranch bunkhouse rather than in the main house. He later moved into the house when his family arrived.

It is possible that the Ostranders did leave the ranch rather hurriedly, and the best reason is the family was in dire financial difficulty in New York. Ostrander had been a great promoter of Texas ranchland sales, having at one time gone all the way to England to encourage buyers to come to Texas. However, when those buyers arrived they expected to be met in New York and given special treatment while looking the land over. In addition, Ostrander also had to tell some of them of the new Texas law forbidding aliens to hold title to land in the state.

Today, many West Texans have forgotten the Ostranders and the Loomis families, but they did bring economic benefits to the area with the lavish spending, the grand mansion that was left behind, and the examples of Eastern culture they set.

Rankin Beach

The Hot Spot of West Texas

LITTLE REMAINS OF RANKIN BEACH, once the exotic playground for thousands of oilfield workers and ranch families in the middle of dry, scorched, windblown West Texas.

Rankin Beach was a glistening white swimming pool and bathhouse complex built 200 yards from a fancy, three-story hotel that rancher-oilman Ira G. Yates constructed in his hometown of Rankin during the roaring 1920s when oilfields suddenly began to spring up for many miles around Upton County. Until early 1927 Rankin was a railroad weigh-station and cattle shipping point. The town had a couple of general merchandise stores, a grocery owned by Yates, and a post office.

When oil was discovered at nearby Texon and the Santa Rita No. 1 spewed thousands of barrels of oil per day, boomers rushed into the area by the thousands, stopping just long enough to throw together clapboard and sheet iron shacks, tents, dugouts, and every other conceivable kind of hovel for shelter. What was for a short time a shantytown quickly became a town with city dimensions and city requirements.

Folks who still remember the oil boom can recall the putt-putt-putt of the piston driven pumps pulling the oil from deep beneath the desert brush. Brilliant flares cast an eerie light over the landscape at night as the unwanted natural gas was burned away, giving the air a sulphur odor and warning that this was "oil country."

"Oil was easy to find," one old-timer recalled. Water was harder to come by. In some places you could pay more for a quart of water than for a gallon of oil. At one time in Rankin and neighboring McCamey and Crane, water sold for $1 a barrel while crude sold for 10 cents a barrel.

This was the general picture of the area when Ira G. Yates got involved. Yates, a grocery store operator, had swapped his store for a Pecos County ranch. Geologists of the day claimed no oil existed west of the Pecos River. Ranchers called the area the "graveyard of a cowman's dreams."

Like many other ranchers needing money, Yates started

YATES VARIETY

the map." The hotel was elegant for its day. Three stories high, constructed of brick and tile, with forty-six guestrooms on the upper floors, of which twenty-three had private baths, the hotel quickly became a hub of the community. The ground floor had a kitchen, dining room, drugstore, barber shop, commissary, and space for commercial offices. Nearby was Scot Skidmore's Plantation Pavilion, a sophisticated eating place with an elegant hardwood dance floor and bandstand. Music and other entertainment blared forth from Skidmore's every night.

selling oil leases on his place. Fortunately for him and hundreds of other landowners, the Yates Ranch became a part of the multibillion-dollar oil producing Yates Field of West Texas—one of the most prolific oil discoveries of the twentieth century. On Friday, January 11, 1985, the Yates Field produced its one-billionth barrel of oil. For more than seventy years, the Yates Field has been one of the largest crude oil reserves in the United States.

After the gigantic oil strike on Yates' land on October 28, 1926, Yates wanted to express confidence in the future of what was once his hometown. He built the Yates Hotel to "put the town on

As summer approached, Yates realized his dream. He built Rankin Beach.

Rankin Beach was a glistening white swimming pool and bathhouse complex located about 200 yards from the hotel. The concrete pool, 120 feet long, 60 feet wide, and 7 feet deep at its deepest end, was surrounded by pure ocean sand that Yates had imported from the Texas Gulf

Coast. Water poured into the pool daily from three giant wells. There were three levels of diving platforms. It was a wonderful mecca for the oilfield workers and ranch families and big-money spenders who came to invest in oil leases. Soon Yates added a roller-skating rink to the complex to provide additional entertainment to the hundreds of people who came daily.

The dance pavilion, with its 60-foot by 60-foot dance floor, was as busy as the swimming pool. The first orchestra to provide music for the dancers was the Alphonso Trent musical ensemble of fifteen musicians. The orchestra was from "back East." Soon, other well-known musical groups were arriving, sent to West Texas direct from the Aragon Ballroom and the Palladium. These big bands were those that country folk tuned to each night on the old Red and Blue radio networks, which featured live, one-hour programs of popular music each night.

Among the big band musicians to play at Rankin and neighboring oil boom towns were Lawrence Welk, New Orleans jazz man Jack Teagarden, and trumpet player Louis Armstrong.

Rankin was quickly becoming a tourist attraction. Tourist trains were assembled on the Kansas City, Mexico, Orient Railroad, taking citizens from San Angelo, Sherwood, Mertzon, Barnhart, Big Lake, Best, and Texon into Rankin for the festivities. Round-trip fare from San Angelo was $4.75, all extras included.

Rankin Beach's popularity quickly spread as oil company moguls learned of the town's possibilities. Hollywood movie stars, famous politicians, and even some foreign dignitaries came to visit the town and its attractions. Some discussed the possibility of settling in Rankin. It appeared that Rankin's future would be bright and very prosperous.

In October 1929 the stock market crash mortally wounded Rankin Beach and thousands of its faithful visitors. The Depression sounded the death knell for Rankin's unusual playground. It has seldom been heard of again, and many present-day Rankin residents are not aware it ever existed.

Part III

Things

Don't Fence Me In

Barbed Wire in Texas

ALONG EVERY HIGHWAY in Texas are miles and miles of fencing—from simple strands of barbed wire tacked to cedar posts to fancy net wire stretched tight enough to play music on. Today's fences also carry warning signs saying "No Trespassing," "Posted," and simply "Stay Out." It wasn't always like this. At one time in the late 1870s, there was one fence between Fort Worth and the Pecos River, and it was designed to turn cattle back as they drifted freely. Drift fences were strictly temporary.

By the 1870s agricultural expansion had swept across the Great Plains. It would have spread even farther except for the lack of fencing materials to protect livestock and crops.

In the Texas Hill Country, especially in and around Mason, are the remnants of stone or rock fences that pioneer settlers labored over for years. Surprisingly, these same fences still hold livestock in check while protecting field crops.

On November 24, 1874, a DeKalb, Illinois, inventor named Joseph F. Glidden was granted a patent for a type of fencing material that consisted of barbs wrapped around a single strand of wire. The barbs were held in place by twisting that strand around another. Glidden's design, called the "Winner," became the most commercially successful barbed wire of the many hundreds of designs created later.

Another inventor, Isaac L. Ellwood, also of DeKalb, patented another type of barbed wire as well, but Ellwood soon concluded that his design was inferior to that of Glidden. Thus, Ellwood and Glidden went into a partnership, which proved extremely rewarding for both men.

In May 1876 Glidden and Ellwood sold their barbed wire patents to a wire manufacturer, Washburn and Moen of Massachusetts. Ellwood remained an active partner in the new company and was named the sole agent and distributor for the South and West.

Washburn and Moen, which was eventually absorbed by the

U.S. Steel Corporation, had successfully acquired all major barbed wire patents. The company would have a near monopoly on this important agriculture product.

Barbed wire came to Texas in 1875 when Henry Sanborn traveled to the Southwest as a representative of Glidden and Ellwood's fencing company. Although he sold the first barbed wire in the state, Sanborn failed to exploit the huge potential market.

Another salesman, John W. "Bet-a-Million" Gates, a former hardware store owner from Illinois, came to Texas in 1876. Inspired by Doc Lighthall's medicine show, Gates in 1878 rented Military Plaza in San Antonio, then Texas's largest city, and constructed a barbed wire corral. He successfully demonstrated to a horrified and disbelieving public that the flimsy-looking wire could hold a milling, snorting, pawing bunch of longhorn cattle. His medicine show salesmanship resulted in orders for more barbed wire than the factory could make.

Gates later touted his barbed wire as "light as air, stronger than whiskey, and cheap as dirt."

Later Gates returned to Illinois and attempted to buy a partnership in the Washburn-Moen company. When his offer was rejected, he quit and went to St. Louis where, in partnership with Alfred Clifford, he built the Southern Wire Company into the largest manufacturer and distributor of "non-patented" barbed wire in the country. In four years, barbed wire had permanently changed land uses and land values in Texas.

Among the first cattlemen to see the benefits of the wire was Charles Goodnight, who fenced his open rangelands along the Palo Duro Canyon. Others quickly followed.

In the summer and fall of 1883, a conflict developed between landless cattlemen who were operating ranches on open range and those who bought barbed wire by the trainload to fence the land to establish themselves permanently. The conflict, later described as the fence cutting war, was precipitated by the drought of 1883, which made it even more difficult for ranchers without land of their own to find grass and water for their cattle.

Right: *Closeup of piece of barbed wire. Photo courtesy* San Angelo Standard-Times.

Most of the larger ranch operators owned or leased the land that they fenced. Others, however, enclosed public land when they fenced their pastures, or strung wire about farms and small ranches that belonged to other people. Fences blocked public roads and in some instances cut off schools and churches and interfered with the delivery of mail. This unwarranted fencing led some men whose land was not actually fenced in to join in nipping their neighbors' wire. As the cutting continued, it became less discriminate. Soon, rougher elements came into the communities. No rancher's fence was safe.

More than half of Texas's counties reported fence cutting. State officials were concerned. Most of the fence cutting was being done in a belt extending through the middle of the state from south to north. The armed bands of fence cutters, calling themselves by such names as the Owls, Blue Devils, or Javelinas, would work at night.

It was not good for a man to be caught with a pair of wire nippers in his saddlebag.

By the fall of 1883, damage from fence cutting in Texas was estimated at $20 million, with Brown County in Central Texas accounting for more than $1 million in losses.

Texas newspapers generally condemned the fence cutters, but several also noted that not all the fencers were free of blame.

The *Fort Worth Gazette* claimed that fence troubles in the state had caused tax valuations to decline by $30 million. The clashes, which

> More than half of Texas's counties reported fence cutting. State officials were concerned. Most of the fence cutting was being done in a belt extending through the middle of the state from south to north. The armed bands of fence

were getting more violent as time went by, were discouraging farming and scaring away prospective new settlers. For a time, politicians shied away from the issue, but on October 15, 1883, Governor John Ireland called a special session of the Texas Legislature to meet on January 8, 1884, to take action on the issue.

Ireland's move was none too soon. Violence was developing all over the state with a number of shootings being reported between fence cutters and landowners.

Wire cutting was first reported in Brown County in August 1883. The *Austin American-Statesman* published a story that reported four miles of fence owned by ranchers Thurmond and Houston in Brown County had been cut by "parties unknown."

"Fence cutting prevails in this

cutters, calling themselves by such names as the Owls, Blue Devils, or Javelinas, would work at night.

It was not good for a man to be caught with a pair of wire nippers in his saddlebag.

section to an alarming extent and if not stopped the rope and mob are liable to be resorted to," the newspaper observed.

In November 1883 rancher L. P. Baugh reported catching eight men cutting his pasture fence on Pecan Bayou. He called the men to stop, having recognized four of them. In reply, the men fired some twenty to thirty shots at Baugh. One fence on the Baugh ranch had

the wire cut between every post for a mile.

According to news reports, the heaviest toll of fence cutting was on the L. P. and W. M. Baugh fences, located on Pecan Bayou and Jim Ned Creek. The Coggin ranch fence also was cut by a large band of cutters in broad daylight the following month. In Brown County alone, forty-five citizens had thirty-two pasture fences cut. These pastures ranged in size from 6 acres to more than 4,800 acres. Many rail fences were torn down or burned, and ranchers were given written warnings that they would be killed if the fences were rebuilt.

One of the largest individual losses occurred in Coke County. Prominent rancher L. B. Harris had fenced twelve sections of land (7,680 acres) on the Colorado River. One night in the fall of 1883 fence cutters cut some forty miles of this fence between every other post.

According to Coke County historian Jessie Newton Yarbrough, the Harrises were getting ready to fence some land about four miles west of the present town of Robert Lee. They had a huge pile of cedar posts—"A pile as high as a two-story house"—and a carload of barbed wire just south of Russell Crossing in a bend of the river when free range advocates put the torch to it. A half-melted spool of barbed wire from that fire is on display in the Coke County Museum.

One of the first to die in the fence cutting war was range detective Ben Warren, who had been hired by Coke County rancher Colonel Thomas L. Odom, to seek out the culprits who had cut fence on the Odom-Wylie Brothers ranch at Fort Chadbourne.

Odom and fellow members of the Coke County cattlemen's association sent Warren to Austin for training. During a meeting between Odom and Warren in the lobby of the Commercial Hotel in Sweetwater the night before the district court convened to investigate the fence cutting situation, someone shot Warren to death through a north window of the hotel. The killer was never caught.

On December 7, 1883, about noon, some riders appeared at the Brown County sheriff's office to report that a large group of men had gathered at the Coggin ranch with intentions of cutting the pasture fences. At the request of the ranch owner, the sheriff and a posse of thirty riders, all heavily armed, rode out to put a stop to the fence cutting.

As a result of the confrontation on the Coggin ranch, the fence cutters threatened to destroy Brownwood—burn it to the ground.

At about 3 o'clock in the morning, it was reported that over 200 fence cutters were headed for town to "lay Brownwood in ashes" and to kill some of its citizens. The townspeople quickly armed themselves and made ready for the attack. The Brownwood Opera House was converted into an arsenal, and messengers were sent out into the country to determine the size of the band coming to attack the town and to alert the country folks. Soon, men were coming from all directions to help defend the community.

Heavily armed men stationed themselves on the rooftops. One old-timer recalled years later that "Uncle Joe" Weakley, pioneer merchant, had sold every firearm he had in stock and all the ammunition. Everyone was convinced, he said, that there would be a real slaughter.

At an early hour the signal was given, and the fence cutters started converging on the town from every direction. Each was armed with a Winchester rifle and pistols. The man heading the fence cutters, J. B. Scruggins of Brown County, came riding in ahead of a group of some twenty men. He was met by Sheriff W. N. "Bill" Adams, who commanded the bunch to lay down their arms so that no one would get killed. The stand-off lasted only a short time before the cutters agreed to put away their weapons.

Sheriff Adams then invited Scruggins and his followers to come into the courthouse to discuss the matter. Adams wanted to know their intentions, and he wanted to know their gripes. A newspaper reporter later wrote, "There were some very violent speeches." One speechmaker, County Judge Charles H. Jenkins, finally stood up and warned the group what would happen if such violence was allowed to happen. His speech quieted the excited crowd.

Finally, a "peace" committee was appointed to meet with the citizens who were in the Opera House. The meeting became known as the Fence-Cutters Convention. Although it appeared toward the end of the convention that there would be no additional wire cutting, it didn't stop. Lawmakers in Austin, pressured by their constituents, made fence cutting a felony, and it was a crime to have a pair of wire cutters or pliers in one's possession.

Alarmed by the violence, Governor Ireland called a special session of the legislature to take action on the fence cutters. The new law, passed in the special session, decreed that all public lands were to be kept open and a gate set up in every third mile of fencing that touched on public roads. Building fences without the consent of the landowners became a misdemeanor. However, the most powerful section of the law declared fence cutting a felony, punishable by one to five years in prison.

When the state law against fence cutting was passed in February 1884, both small and large landowners were relieved. However, the law did not stop fence cutting completely.

A band of some eight to ten men continued to snip the fences of Brown County ranchers Lev P. Baugh and his brother, W. M. "Morg"

Baugh. The brothers continued to hunt down the culprits and caught some of the men in the act of cutting fence.

The Baughs presented evidence to a Brown County grand jury, which eventually indicted ten men for fence cutting in March 1885. However, the cases never went to court. A Bell County judge dismissed the charges against the men in June 1888.

There were no winners in the barbed wire war. The fence cutters never served time in jail, and the ranchers had spent huge sums of money building and repairing fences. However, fear had receded in the country. People felt safe to go to church without having to tote their shotguns, Winchesters, and pistols, and there were no more night patrols.

Now, the big job was for the ranchers and farmers and citizens to learn to live with barbed wire.

Saving a Train Load of Mohair

800,000 Pounds Damaged by Floodwaters

MOHAIR, THE SILKY FLEECE from Angora goats, has been a cash crop for Texas Hill Country ranchers and stock farmers for generations. Although early-day ranchers were hesitant to admit that they kept goats on their ranches, preferring to be grouped with their cattlemen neighbors, the goats paid many feed bills for the other animals, bought groceries, and even put Junior through college.

However, mohair has always been a "feast or famine" product, bringing huge sums of money some years, and being near worthless on the world market at other times. As a result, many ranchers and others would speculate on the value of the mohair, keeping it stored in community warehouses until the price would go up.

Several years ago I was hired to write a history of the Texas Sheep and Goat Raisers' Association. The book covered activities of the organization and its membership over an eighty-year period. Most of the members were sheep men, but many of the organization's early leaders were goat men.

In early 1999 I received a letter from a Virginia woman inquiring about the validity of a story that had been passed down in her family concerning a "shipload of mohair" that had nearly been destroyed at a tremendous financial loss. We later talked on the telephone concerning this incident. I was curious about the story since I had not heard about it during the fifteen months that I worked on the industry history book. The only thing I had to go on in tracking the story was the name of her grandfather, Frank Montague Sr. of Bandera, Texas.

The time was 1932. The Great Depression had staggered the country's economy, and thousands of people were out of work. Many had lost all their life savings. Livestock prices were at an all-time low. Animals could not be sold at market because there was no demand for them.

During the fall of 1932, hard rains fell across the western areas of Texas. The wet weather and subsequent cold weather indirectly helped goat producers out of their dilemma. Thousands of goats, freshly shorn of their protective hair, died by the thousands as they chilled down or froze to death.

According to newspaper reports from that time, in San Angelo alone over 1,500 goats were butchered and fed to the needy, either as fresh meat or put up in cans and distributed by members of the fire department. The fire chief, a man named Parker, directed his firefighters in butchering the goats and helping to distribute the meat. The work was done for free, and the goats were donated to the needy by a number of pioneer ranchers, including the Cargile brothers, Sol Mayer and son, Roy Hudspeth, Fayette Tankersley, Abe Mayer, Bob Hewitt, Hub Noelke, and others. The same thing was done in other Texas towns. As a result, the goat numbers plunged and the mohair production fell to record low tonnages.

However, there was still thousands of tons of mohair in storage in warehouses all over the central part of the state. Growers, accustomed to keeping the mohair until prices improved, found themselves in serious financial straits. Many had to sell at whatever prices they could get. Adult mohair eventually sold for as low as a nickel a pound, but averaged eight cents a pound during 1932-33. The better quality hair from young goats would bring perhaps 12 to 15 cents a pound if a buyer could be found.

For persons with good credit, investing in mohair or wool in those days could mean a future bonanza. Warehouse operators

> As an example of this speculative buying, warehouseman Jake Schwartz of Uvalde sent a telegram to then Vice President John Nance Garner in Washington, D.C. that he could sell Garner 100,000

bought lots of mohair at cheap prices because the small ranchers needed money. If they could hold the mohair long enough, it could mean huge profits.

As an example of this speculative buying, warehouseman Jake Schwartz of Uvalde sent a telegram to then Vice President John Nance Garner in Washington, D.C. that he could sell Garner 100,000 pounds of mohair for 17 cents a pound. The purchase was approved, and six months later the mohair sold for 36 cents a pound, resulting in a profit of some $19,000.

Another speculative venture nearly led to disaster. This involved the Virginia woman's grandfather, Frank Montague Sr., and his partner, Peter Ingenhuett of Comfort.

The men bought 800,000 pounds of mohair in 1935 at very

pounds of mohair for 17 cents a pound. The purchase was approved, and six months later the mohair sold for 36 cents a pound, resulting in a profit of some $19,000.

depressed prices. Among the warehousemen who sold mohair to the Montague-Ingenhuett combine was the late Lucius M. "Mickey" Stephens of Lometa, in Lampasas County.

According to Stephens, the mohair accumulation was transported to Houston by truck and railroad car to be warehoused at the Port of Houston until sold to mills either in the U.S. or Europe. The mohair was put in the Manchester Terminal, located right on the ship channel. Tragedy struck in 1938 when the biggest flood in Houston history pushed the ship channel out of its banks, flooding hundreds of warehouses and homes. The Manchester Terminal was flooded, and hundreds of bags of mohair were saturated with water or washed away. For Montague and Ingenhuett, it was serious crying time.

The late Texas Congressman O. Clark Fisher of Junction, who represented the entire Angora goat producing region of Texas, recalled in his book *The Speaker of Nubbin Ridge* that cash in large amounts was very hard to come by, and the two partners had to come up with a plan to save their investment.

Two San Antonio banks came to the men's rescue. Soon, it was determined that much of the mohair was covered by insurance, although no premium had been paid by the men nor did they have an insurance policy in hand.

The mohair was under water for about 48 hours before the water receded. Many bags of the fiber had floated downstream.

Flooded roads delayed Montague's arrival in Houston. He

contacted Tucker Blaine Insurance Agency, which represented a New York insurance company. He was assured that he had insurance coverage on the mohair. When the insurance people learned that the mohair was covered by water, they turned the salvage efforts over to Montague.

Montague rounded up all the young Negro boys he could find and paid them 50 cents a sack for all the mohair they could recover from downstream. He also contacted the Missouri-Pacific Railroad Company. There were no scouring plants in Texas, and he had to ship the mohair to Boston to be washed and dried if it was to be salvaged. Time was of the essence. Mohair fleeces could sour from being wet. It was a critical moment.

According to Stephens, Montague arranged with the railroad to take the wet bags of mohair to Boston and give the shipment the "Red Ball treatment." When he was assured that the railroad could provide express shipment, he asked for the biggest and fastest locomotive to pull the train, and passenger trains due to run on the same track were put on hold to allow the freight to move down the track without slowing down. In addition, Montague gave each of the train crewmen a $100 tip to keep the train moving as fast as possible. He went along for the ride, sitting in the cupola of the caboose.

As the train left Houston, Montague told Stephens that he could see "steam rising" out of the cattle cars that were used to haul the wet mohair. Fortunately for Montague, it was wintertime. By the time the high-speed freight train reached Arkansas, a severe freeze was taking place, so the bags of wet mohair froze solid. It was a stroke of luck because the frozen mohair did not sour and mildew. When the train reached its destination in Boston, work crews had to use crowbars to pry the frozen bags of mohair apart in order to unload them at the scouring plants. Montague remained in Boston for nearly three months to oversee the scouring of the mohair and repacking. While there he was able to find buyers for the huge accumulation.

Later, Montague went to New York City to settle his claim with the insurance firm. Montague's son, Frank Jr., recalled what happened there.

"My father told me he was very nervous until he got his hands on the insurance check. He said after the bills for handling the mohair were considered and approved, the insurance executive told Montague it was customary to "go out to lunch." But Montague was not in the mood for a meal. He thanked the executive but told him he was not hungry. Then the executive offered Montague a drink of liquor to celebrate the occasion. He also refused the drink. When the executive pulled the check from his desk, Montague breathed a sigh of relief.

"I think I am feeling better," Montague told the insurance man. "I think I will take a small snort of what's in that bottle, and I will join you for lunch."

After Montague received the check, the insurance man said, "We don't underestimate you Texans. It takes us two months to settle a damage claim for a coop of turkeys. Your claim has been settled in thirty minutes."

The New York insurance company had good reason to be pleased with Montague's work in salvaging the huge tonnage of mohair. The loss to the insurance company was reduced by 18 percent under what it would have been except for Montague's quick action.

Montague continued in the wool and mohair business with his partner, Peter Ingenhuett, for thirty years. They mutually dissolved their partnership a number of years later.

Painted Rocks on the Concho

A Major Rock Art Site in Texas

ABOUT TWO MILES NORTHWEST of the community of Paint Rock in Concho County is one of the major rock art sites in the state and perhaps the premier site in Central Texas.

There are an estimated 1,500 paintings, or pictographs, spread out over rock cliffs stretching a half-mile or more along the north side of the river. These cliffs of limestone are up to seventy feet high and are located from 150 to 200 yards from the river.

According to researchers, there appears to be little connection between the painted rocks in Concho County and those found in the Lower Pecos region, the closest neighboring site of early Native American artwork.

The painted rocks are located on private land owned by Kay and Fred Campbell. The site, which has been in the Campbell-Sims family since it was purchased in 1878 by D. E. Sims, was a noted camping ground for Indians over several hundred years.

Experts say the range of time covered by the pictographs is fairly long, extending from the dim prehistoric to the early historic period. Dating the pictographs in a more precise manner is impossible, but some shards of Leon Plain ceramics and burned rock middens suggest that some of the paintings could be over 1,000 years old.

The Campbells recognize the importance of the artifacts on the ranch, and both have acted as protective custodians of the site for years. They give occasional guided tours to interested groups on request.

Most of the figures at Paint Rock are generally small and appear to have been painted as individual designs rather than being a part of a giant mural. Geometric designs, animal and human figures, and handprints are the most predominant. The colors are: orange, red, yellow, black, and white. Experts who have examined the pictographs say the red, yellow, and orange pigments are derived from oxides of iron containing ochers, while the black and white colors come from carbon and chalk. All these materials to mix the colors are available in the near vicinity of the cliffs.

During a visit to the pictographs, landowner Kay Campbell noted that some of the designs and figures depict scenes that are historic in nature. Horses, a devil, and a mission recall the early Spanish presence at Santa Cruz de San Saba Mission, which was located about forty miles away near present-day Menard. The mission, established in 1757 for the Lipan Apaches, was later destroyed and the priests murdered. The mission is depicted as a long rectangular building with two cross-topped towers. Close by, black smoke billows up near the mission, perhaps commemorating its destruction in 1758.

Another pictograph reveals the kidnapping of Alice Todd, in 1865, who was taken from her home near Mason when she was just fourteen years old. There are pictographs of two crossed lances

Above: *Closeup of sun dagger shining on painted rocks in Concho County. Photo courtesy Campbell family.*

and two long-haired scalps, which record the killing of Alice's mother and a slave woman. Near this pictograph is another of a woman drawn in a horizontal form, a typical depiction of captivity. These scenes record the raid on

Above: *Some of the painted rocks in Concho County. Photo courtesy Campbell family.*

the Todd family's farm and the kidnapping of the young girl. Alice Todd was never heard of again. Some say the story of the Todd girl being taken by the Comanches is the basis of the book *The Searchers,* which was later made into a very successful movie starring John Wayne.

The painted rocks area has never been excavated by professionals, and there are few published descriptions of the site, usually limited to stories published in popular journals, travel magazines, and newspapers. Those who have studied the Indian rock art wonder why the spot was chosen for such decorations or what the symbols really mean. Unlike the rock shelters in the Lower Pecos and along the Rio Grande, the Paint Rock area never served the Indians as a semi-permanent place of abode. Rather, bands apparently stopped to camp or to rest and water their horses. Thus, the paintings were left by Indians who put them on the rocks as a way to pass the time.

In 1934 Lula and Forrest Kirkland visited the site and made watercolor paintings of many of the designs and figures, which eventually were published in a book about Texas Indian rock art. However, the Kirklands were unable to provide an interpretation of the drawings because many had been vandalized over the years. According to records from Fort Concho, one of Texas's most active frontier posts, soldiers and their families used to make outings to the painted rocks. Many left their names and dates on the rocks alongside the Indian markings.

In recent years the painted rocks have drawn the interest of R. Robert Robbins, an archaeoastronomer with the University of Texas Astronomy Department at Austin. He has reported on the results of nearly two years of observations of an unusual seasonal interplay of sunlight discovered among many of the pictographs.

Dr. Robbins was alerted to this curious solar behavior by the owners, Fred and Kay Campbell, when they found that dramatic daggers of sunlight strike the rocks in the summer and winter solstice and shine on pictographs clearly drawn on the rocks to receive them. Further, Robbins relates, these daggers of light reach their maximum altitude in the rocks at a time that agrees with solar apparent time to within a few minutes.

Robbins noted in his report that the so-called sun daggers strongly suggest that the Indians using the Concho River site were constructing and making use of seasonal markers that exhibit a higher degree of calendrical skills than has been attributed to them.

"This solar timepiece would allow the various hunter-gatherer tribes to successfully assemble and conduct necessary business, as well as seek shelter from the winter," he noted.

The site of the painted rocks would be an ideal place to winter, with the long, tall bluff facing south providing a natural shelter against the cold, crisp north winds. During the summer the site would provide shade and

> The painted rocks area has never been excavated by professionals, and there are few published descriptions of the site, usually limited to stories published in popular journals, travel magazines, and newspapers.

breezes created by the Concho River, just 100 yards away.

According to D. E. Sims, grandfather of Kay Campbell, who bought the ranch in 1878 and had many opportunities to communicate with local Indians, the "shield" painting signifies a council meeting conducted by five bands of Indians to divide the hunting lands. The number 5 does appear twice in the painting design. Who were these five bands of Indians? Tribes that used the camping place included Comanche, Lipan Apache, Kiowa, Tonkawa, and the Jumanos. The Tonks and the Jumanos came into the territory much earlier.

Rollins made his first report of the sun daggers in January 1999. He plans on doing additional studies and sharing his findings with the American Astronomical Society.

A Wild and Woolly Land Rush

THE SCHLEICHER COUNTY COURTHOUSE was only a three-room frame building when Eldorado became the scene of three land rushes in which guns were drawn, fists flew, and people battled for the right to buy cheap school lands.

The moviemakers have filmed more than once their idea of what a land rush was like during the pioneer days, focusing on wild and scary, helter-skelter races of people riding in wagons, buggies, buckboards, and on horses and mules speeding across the prairie toward rich pasturelands ready to be settled and tilled.

Although this kind of rush actually happened in 1889 when certain lands were opened for development in Oklahoma Indian Territory, land rushes of a different kind were taking place in Texas.

Schleicher County and Eldorado have been the site of three land rushes. The first only a few weeks after the county was organized in 1901 and two others in 1905 and 1910. The first land rush at Eldorado resulted in one of West Texas's largest ranches, the Vermont, to eventually be broken up into some twenty or more smaller ranches.

The Schleicher County land rushes did not result in any hell-for-leather wagon and buggy races, but the drama and the suspense was just as potent. Six-shooters were drawn and cocked, threats were made, and the tension around the three-room clapboard courthouse in the center of this early-day community was as taut as a fresh-stretched barbed wire fence. There was no wholesale bloodletting, but some noses got smashed, knuckles got skinned, and more than one shin got kicked.

In the first rush, the land came on the market at 12:01 a.m. on August 22, 1901, according to an early account by the late F. C. Bates Jr., the first county clerk who had to take the money and applications. Bates related that the first tract of land contained about 100 sections or more, the leases on such having expired at midnight, August 21.

"I opened the doors to the

clerk's office to receive the applications, and the surge against the little frame courthouse was so great it shook the entire building," Bates wrote in 1930.

Bates had a harrowing night before the rush began. One man, a 200-pounder, pushed "a big .45-caliber six-shooter in my face" and demanded that his application and money be processed ahead of the many others standing in line. But Sam Littlepage, one of eight men deputized especially for the event, came up and struck the man "between the eyes" with another big pistol, saying at the same time "put up your pistol, be a man, and wait your turn in line," Bates recalled years later.

During the first filing, more than $2,000 in cash was collected. The money came from down payments on the lands being offered and was to be sent to Austin. Land was bringing $1 per acre, with 1/40th paid in advance, the remainder at 3 percent interest over a 40-year period. Bates wrote that he planned to bring the money to a San Angelo bank but learned before the trip that an outlaw named Oscar Finley was planning to rob him near Christoval. The money was taken instead to Sonora under heavy armed guard.

The late Christopher Columbus Doty, the county's first tax collector, served as official timer during the first land rush. He also sat on a bushel basket holding the money and guarded it with a Winchester rifle across his lap.

"Those were pretty busy times," Doty recalled in later years. "I had to set down the exact

> One man, a 200-pounder, pushed "a big .45-caliber six-shooter in my face" and demanded that his application and money be processed ahead of the many others standing in line. But Sam Littlepage, one of eight men

time and second that we received the claim. A second often meant that a fellow got or lost his land."

According to Doty's recollections, there were two distinct factions gathered when the filing date came: cattlemen opposing incoming settlers. The cattlemen owned some of the land and held leases on adjoining school lands that were put up for sale. When their leases expired, the cattlemen wanted to buy the land so their holdings would not be divided or cut up. The cattlemen did not care for the settlers and ridiculed them for their folly in believing that a man could make a living on only four sections of land (2,560 acres). The cattlemen called the settlers "one gallus fellows."

Doty said, "When we opened up, men rolled, crawled, and

deputized especially for the event, came up and struck the man "between the eyes" with another big pistol, saying at the same time "put up your pistol, be a man, and wait your turn in line," Bates recalled years later.

walked on the shoulders of others to make their way towards the slot in the door. When one man was crowded out of the line, he passed his roll of money and his claim application to somebody else on his side.

"When the crowding became too great, Winchesters were poked through the door slots and the men were ordered to 'back away or we will have to shoot,'"

Doty recalled.

During a later land rush, Doty said the county sheriff had, for some reason, failed to disarm the crowd waiting to file claims. During the rushing and pushing and shoving, Doty said he heard the click of a six-shooter being cocked.

"Immediately, about twenty-five others followed suit," Doty said. Trouble seemed to be inevitable, but a deputy sheriff stepped up to the crowd and said the first man to shoot his pistol would be a "dead man." Bloodshed was averted by only seconds.

Doty said about sixty men had come from adjoining Irion County to file on the school lands being offered for sale by the county. "They had their faces painted yellow to distinguish them from the home crowd." Doty said Schleicher County men resented this maneuver and managed to fight them off and get the land.

The land rush events even drew the attention of children as the youngsters started playing "land rush" at school. One boy got his arm broken in a make-believe rush for the slot in the door.

The last land rush in Schleicher County came in 1905. A man

named William E. Murphy and his eldest son, Tom, had camped in front of the courthouse door for several days. Shortly before the doors opened at 9:01 a.m. the pair got help from some rancher friends and were successful in filing on some three sections of land.

A man named Don McCormick recalled in a newspaper interview in August 1962 that he witnessed the last land rush while going to school.

"Some of the young folks may think they have seen some rough play on the football field, but that is nothing compared with the land rush," McCormick said. "I never saw any gunplay, but I did see a lot of men get some rough treatment, including some fistfights."

When settlers started filing on school lands situated in the eighty-section Vermont Ranch pasture, the giant ranching company that had been started in 1884 by a group of Winsdor County, Vermont men started to deteriorate as a single land holding. The ranch had originally consisted of more than 25,000 acres, which the men bought for $14,502 from various railroad companies. The railroad companies had been given the land by the state of Texas for building rail lines in various parts of the state. The land had been divided into alternate sections; the railroads having one section and the state having one section adjoining it. This state land, later given to the schools, was the parcels sold to settlers during the rushes.

Before the Vermont Ranch was broken up by the land rushes, the ranch carried more than 5,000 head of sheep and several thousand head of cattle and horses. The first town in Schleicher County was located on the Vermont Ranch. The town, called Verand, had a stage station, hotel, store, school, and several other buildings and was situated about a quarter-mile from the Vermont Ranch headquarters. The few families that lived in Verand moved to Eldorado when it was started in 1895. The Verand town site was abandoned.

The land laws of 1901 and 1903 caused much dissatisfaction and conflicts over the filing of school land. The law made land rushes possible and tended to encourage the old conflicts between cattlemen and settlers.

In March 1903 a concurrent resolution was passed in the Texas

Legislature which stated that it had been reliably reported that a rush on the clerk's office in some counties was impending and that armed persons were encamped near these various clerks' offices prepared to interrupt and prevent the fair and impartial award of these lands as intended by the existing land laws. The resolution held up the sale of the land for ninety days but did not stop the land rushes.

The law was finally changed in 1905 so that the school land was sold to the highest bidder and all sales were made directly by the Commissioner of the General Land Office at Austin and not through the local county clerk where the land was situated. The new law removed the occasion for land rushes, and they became a thing of the past.

Nazi Terrorism

Reminders of Brutality Found in Texas

EVEN AFTER MORE THAN SIXTY YEARS since the outbreak of World War II, there are still reminders of Nazi terrorism in areas of Texas where Nazi soldiers beat, tortured, intimidated, and killed people in places like Brady, Wharton, Ganado, and Palacios. It was a cruel time in which German prisoners of war were being held by the thousands in camps stretching from the Texas Panhandle to the lower Rio Grande Valley.

The victims of the crimes by some of Hitler's finest troops were not Texans; they were fellow German soldiers who were not card-carrying, fanatic members of the Nazi Party.

The Germans—Nazi and non-Nazi alike—were captured by Allied forces on battlefields in North Africa, Italy, France, and elsewhere from 1942 through 1946 and brought to Texas for confinement in the seventy or so POW camps scattered across the state.

When the United States went to war in 1941, one of the last considerations given by the war planners was what to do with enemy prisoners of war. The nation had never held large numbers of foreign prisoners and certainly was not prepared for the many tasks involved, such as registration, food, clothing, housing, entertainment, and even re-education. Prepared or not, the U.S. was soon on the receiving end of massive waves of German and Italian POWs. More than 150,000 men arrived in the U.S. after the surrender of General Erwin Rommel's Afrika Korps in April 1943. Soon an average of 20,000 new POWs were arriving each month. From the Normandy invasion in June 1944 through December, 30,000 new prisoners arrived each month. When the war was over, there were 425,000 enemy prisoners in 511 main and branch camps throughout the U.S.

Texas, with more available space and curiously, better climate, had approximately twice as many POW camps as any other state. The Geneva Convention of 1929 specifies that POWs be moved to a climate similar to that where they are captured, thus it was believed that the climate of Texas was similar to that in North Africa. At the end of the war,

Texas had 78,900 POWs, mainly Germans, at fourteen military installations: Camp Barkeley near Abilene, Camp Bowie at Brownwood, Camp Fannin in Smith County, Camp Hood at Killeen, Camp Howze in Cooke County, Camp Hulen near Matagorda Bay, Camp Maxey in Lamar County, Camp Swift at Bastrop, Camp Wolters at Mineral Wells, Fort Bliss at El Paso, Fort Brown at Brownsville, Fort Crockett at Galveston, Fort D. A. Russell at Marfa, and Fort Sam Houston in San Antonio.

There also were seven base camps that were set up especially for POWs. They were located at Brady, Hearne, Hereford, Huntsville, McLean, Mexia, and Wallace, in Galveston County.

The Brady Internment Camp, located about two miles east of Brady, was expressly used for Germans transferred from other camps in the U.S. where they had reputations as troublemakers. The Brady camp opened in September 1943 and was deactivated soon after May 7, 1945. The camp had a capacity for 3,000 prisoners held

Below: *Main entrance with old guardhouse to Brady POW camp. Photo courtesy* San Angelo Standard-Times.

behind double rows of barbed wire fencing. The camp was scattered over 360 acres of land and included some 200 buildings. The largest structure was a 150-bed hospital. An army detachment of about 500 men operated the camp and made up the guard units.

The barracks and mess halls were mostly constructed of frame lumber and sheetrock on a concrete slab floor, covered by tarpaper. A potbellied stove sat in the center of each building. In fact, the only real difference in the POW camps and American army training facilities were the

Above: *Foundation of Brady POW camp headquarters building. Photo courtesy* San Angelo Standard-Times.

watchtowers located along the double barbed-wire fence, floodlights, and at some camps, dog patrols.

Discipline among the prisoners was rigidly enforced by German officers and sergeants. Although they appeared to be uncomfortable, some people believed the camps were too good for the captives, and many Texans called the local camps the "Fritz Ritz."

With millions of American men

in uniform, there was a serious labor shortage so the War Department approved a major program to allow farmers to utilize the POWs. Grateful farmers and ranchers paid the government the prevailing wage of $1.50 per day, and the prisoner was paid 80 cents in canteen coupons. The difference was sent to the U.S. treasury to pay for the POW program. Under the Geneva Convention, officers were not required to work, thus most German officers refused to volunteer. However, many of the soldiers, with farming backgrounds before being conscripted into the German army, were eager to work. In Texas, the POWs picked peaches and citrus fruits, harvested rice, cut wood, baled hay, threshed grain, gathered pecans, and chopped huge amounts of cotton. The usual day started with reveille at 5:45 a.m., and lights were out by 10 p.m. Between those times the POWs worked, took care of their own needs, or perhaps participated in classes and sports. However, the outside opportunity to work was well received. In some cases the prisoners and their employers made long-lasting friendships.

But in camps like the Brady facility, Nazis would terrorize their own soldiers into obeying such Nazi commands as not working, breaking tools, and other acts of hostility.

At Brady, most all of the trouble was instigated by former members of the Nazi SS, which was noted for its brutality to both civilians and opposing soldiers. One such incident happened in May 1945, when the U.S. War Department issued an order that all German POWs cease using the Nazi straight-arm salute. Six former SS members succeeded in convincing one of the three prisoner compounds to remain loyal to Hitler and continue using the prohibited salute.

The camp commander, Army Colonel Robert C. Saxton, who was familiar with "belly wrinkling" tactics, ordered the removal of all food from the compound kitchen, put the compound's 1,229 prisoners on a bread and water diet, and ordered there be no hot water for bathing, no heat, no lights, no recreational facilities, and no work details. Within a week the prisoners had discontinued the Nazi salute.

Most camps received little media attention in those days. In fact, the Army kept camp operations and reports of Nazi terrorism secret for years after the war ended.

Escape attempts were made, but most were unsuccessful. However, one escape did work for three prisoners at Brady. The men, members of Rommel's Afrika Korps, escaped on Sunday April 16, 1944. Nine days later, on the morning of April 25, a ranch woman near Rocksprings heard a knock on her door and found a haggard-looking man holding a canteen and speaking German. She quickly closed and locked the door and called the Border Patrol, which arrested the three escapees nearby a short time later. The men had successfully walked from Brady to near Rocksprings, a distance of more than 100 miles.

The prisoners faced insurmountable odds against escaping successfully—the vast countryside, the language difference, and the absence of an underground railway or safe haven. Records show that only twenty-one prisoners escaped, the majority from Hearne and Mexia, and that every escapee was caught within three weeks.

Most escapes were rather comical affairs; unlike the Brady escape in which the men suffered extreme physical exhaustion, hunger, and thirst. A prisoner at Mexia called for help after having been chased up a tree by an angry Brahma bull. Three others, from Hearne, were found in a makeshift raft paddling on the Brazos River hoping to sail back to Germany.

In recent years researchers have found that the American army was aware of Nazi activity in the camps but was never able to prevent Nazi groups, which included members of the notorious Gestapo, from exerting control over other prisoners. The Nazis set up a clandestine communications network that reached from camp to camp—and even all the way back to Germany—which they used to direct beatings, intimidation, and murders of non-Nazis.

According to researcher Richard P. Walker, who worked on a lengthy report of German POW activities in the 1970s, there was quite a bit of intimidation by the Nazis, because they wanted to control all the reading material and sometimes even the work schedules that could lead to prisoner strikes.

One non-Nazi POW was murdered. He had been born in New York but moved to Germany and joined the army after being influenced by an American pro-Nazi group. The victim was captured in North Africa and sent to the POW camp at Huntsville where he became a collaborator with the Americans. The Nazis found out that he was spying on them. A group of them, about ten, sneaked into the compound where he was being held and beat him to death.

In another case, a German prisoner was foolish enough to make a speech in the barracks questioning Hitler's leadership. He was warned by the Nazis that they were going to get his parents back in Germany. Sure enough, about six months later the foolish prisoner received word from Germany that his parents and little sister had been brutalized and persecuted by the Nazis. When the prisoner found out that his family had suffered because of his barracks oratory, he committed suicide.

After the war ended, the prisoners were readied for repatriation. They were moved from the smaller camps to the military installations at Forts Bliss, Sam Houston, and Hood where they were returned to Europe at the rate of about 50,000 per month. Most were used to help rebuild war-damaged France and England before their ultimate return to Germany.

As the POWs left Texas by the trainload, the camps began to close. In Hearne, Brady, and several others, the camps were put up for public auction. Other facilities were utilized by schools, housing developers, the Texas National Guard, and the Bastrop camp was developed into an $11 million medium-security federal prison for first offenders.

Today, only a guardhouse and a few old tattered buildings remain of Brady's POW camp.

The Freighter and the Madstone

THERE ISN'T MUCH LEFT of Stiles to show for its prominence except its old abandoned courthouse and cemetery located about a mile away. However, the once busy Reagan County community will always have a place in the hearts of western lore lovers because of the "madstone."

The story of the madstone is supposed to be true, but whether it is or not it makes for a western spellbinder that has caught the fancy of cowboy storytellers since the trail driving days.

San Angelo, once a buffalo hide town and scabtown to nearby Fort Concho, used to have a lot of freighters. Among them were A. J. Fry, Bill Latham, M. E. Faubion, J. R. Finch, R. I. and Jimmy Rushing, Arilius Latham, J. C. Newton, Fulton Key, Frank Hickam, John Robertson, and a man named Will Pool. The madstone story centers around an event that happened to Pool when he passed through Stiles en route to San Angelo with a load of stock salt for the Harris Brothers.

According to the story, a number of hospitable citizens of the Reagan County community had insisted that Pool attend a dance, rather than make his teams ready for the long trip to San Angelo. About an hour before sundown, Pool made camp, hobbled out all but the trimmest of his work-horses, which he saddled, and took off for the Stiles courthouse where the big dance was being held.

As was customary in those days, there was plenty of food and drink at the dance and the affair lasted well into the night. In fact, it was nearly dawn when the tired but happy freighter returned to his camp. Pool quickly crawled into his bedroll to get a couple of hours sleep before hitching the teams and starting out for San Angelo with the load of salt. He was quickly awakened, however, by a piercing pain in his hand. A pole-cat, or skunk as some call it, had bitten his hand and was sucking his blood. He slung the skunk off his hand, but before he or his dog could kill it, the varmint scampered away and went into a deep hole.

"I wonder if that polecat had hydraphoby?" Pool asked himself. Not wanting to take a chance, he saddled his horse and returned to Stiles where he had old Doc Wittaker lance and cauterize the wound. Then the doctor applied his madstone, but it dropped right off the wounded area. Pool wasn't too impressed and called the doctor's madstone "just an old flat rock."

As Pool headed his freight wagon and team toward Cedar Canyon, he became more worried about the wound on his hand, but he knew he could do nothing about it until he got back to San Angelo from the Harris Ranch. As soon as he unloaded the stock salt, he made fast tracks for the town on the Concho River.

When he arrived at the Concho Street wagon yard, he hit the ground running in search of a madstone.

"Yes, there is a woman in town who has one," he learned from a townsman. He hurried to her little adobe house to find her.

The woman said she believed she could help him out of his predicament. She pulled out a puffy-looking thing about an inch long that had been taken from a blacktail deer. When the woman applied the madstone to the skunk bite on Pool's hand, the madstone clung to it for fourteen hours. After taking the madstone off and boiling it in milk, she replaced it on the wound. This time it stuck for three hours before finally dropping off.

The woman, a Mexican healer, wouldn't let Pool or anyone else touch the stone or handle it in any way. Will Pool went away from her house satisfied that the madstone had saved his life.

Madstones apparently are for real, and the use of such stones many years ago to stop the spread of the rabies disease was more prevalent than first believed.

The story about the San Angelo freighter who had been bitten by a skunk drew lots of attention from folks all over western Texas.

Chic and Dorothy Conrad of San Angelo provided the details of a similar situation that happened to her great-great-grandfather, Warren Angus Ferris, a pioneer surveyor who eventually was asked to plot out the town of Warwick, now a place called Dallas.

Ferris's plight was first detailed in his diaries and later included in a story about madstones that appeared in *True West Magazine* in 1966. Photos of several kinds of madstones were included with the article, courtesy of the Smithsonian Institution in Washington, D.C.

According to the Conrads, Ferris was bitten on the leg by a mad raccoon that had gotten into his home. Two family dogs that fought the varmint were subsequently infected and had to be destroyed.

Ferris sought help and found a madstone in the possession of John Favens, who lived on the west bank of the Trinity River. Ferris's story gives considerable detail on how he believed the porous stone worked its magic in cleansing the wound.

"During the time it was attached to the bite, the evaporating water could be seen as if it was boiling at every tube, and I could feel a distinct burning sensation in the wound such as I presume would be induced by a minute blister of flies," Ferris noted. He later speculated that the rabies virus was drawn from the wound by the porous stone producing a vacuum in its openings, caused by the hot water evaporating, because the virus had little or no affinity for the flesh and blood of the wound, but it did have a strong chemical affinity for something contained in the madstone.

Onions Bring in a Railroad

Eye-Watering Veggie Helps San Saba Grow

PEELING AND DICING ONIONS is not a pleasant chore while working in the kitchen, but the bulb-like plant with the powerful odor seems to make cornbread dressing taste better, and some bean dishes are helped considerably if cooked with a few onion slivers mixed in. Without onions, McDonalds would never have been able to sell all those zillions of hamburgers. Onions have had a major influence on West Texans, from pioneer days to modern times.

Few people know that the pungent, eye-watering vegetable played a major role in bringing a railroad to a big area of Central Texas.

When holidays and other special occasions roll around and we do a lot of extra cooking in our household, my job is peeling the onions. I don't mind, unless the onions are particularly juicy, which results in making my eyes burn and my nose run. Sinus trouble seems to leave at that point. There are ways to keep from crying while peeling onions—if you do it under a water spigot, wear a surgical mask, rubber gloves, and hold your breath. I just do it the hard way, stopping periodically to run outside into the fresh air.

In pioneer days, onions and other wild vegetable-like plants helped keep scurvy from putting soldiers in the post hospital, according to records at San Angelo's Fort Concho National Historic Site. Scurvy is an illness caused by a lack of Vitamin C in the diet, resulting in weakness, anemia, spongy gums, and bleeding from the mucous membranes.

A trial crop of onions won a branch line of the Santa Fe Railroad for the Central Texas area, including San Saba, Richland Springs, Brady, and Eden.

For twenty-five years people living in the San Saba River Valley had been seeking rail service. The San Saba area was drawing settlers to the valley before the Civil War, and for many years the town was a chief gateway into far West Texas. A town can really thrive with a railroad, but San Saba folks had to haul their goods some twenty miles or more by wagon from Lometa.

In 1904 a man named F. G. Pettibone, vice president and general manager of Santa Fe Railroad, sent Professor L. C. Hill to the town to look things over. Hill was a horticulturist, and his job was to talk to the people and tell them what a railroad expected to find when it built a new line. Hill asked the local folks what they had to haul out on the line? "Cattle," they said, noting that the animals had been trailed out of the valley to market for more than twenty years.

Hill said that was nice, but cattle could be driven to another rail line if the sellers did not want to do business with the Santa Fe. He wanted to know what kind of field products were available, something that could not pick up and walk away to another line.

San Saba farmers were producing all sorts of things but mostly for their own use and for the local market. They had good luck growing pecans, some fruits, cabbage, cotton, tomatoes, and feed grain, but they did not know if they could produce enough to fill a trainload each week during a season.

"Show me," said Hill. "Let us see what you can do. Try onions. They are easy to grow and easy to haul to the railroad by wagon."

The following spring farmers and home gardeners planted onions. Everyone had an onion patch; even town lots and backyards were converted into onion beds.

That August the farmers started digging their onions, and wagonload after wagonload made the twenty-mile journey to Lometa to meet the train. The whole onion crop that year was forty carloads, not counting the railcars of cotton, cabbage, pecans, tomatoes, and watermelons that were shipped to market.

Not too long ago, my friend Red Cheek, a dandy storyteller who grew up in the cedar breaks in San Saba County, recalled when he worked for a farmer harvesting onions on a place between Bend and Colony. He remembered that the work was all "stoop labor," bending over the plants in the fields, cutting off the tops with a makeshift sickle made from a knife tied to a broomstick, then gathering the onions after they were plowed up. The pay was "by the row" then by the basket. Later the onions were taken into the shade of a big tree and sorted for size and put into fifty-pound sacks.

One day when the crew had finished, Cheek's father told the farmer to deduct $1 for one of the bags of onions. The farmer offered to give the workers onions from the piles of odd shaped, too small onions that had been sorted out.

"Take all the onions you can use," the farmer said, thus all the Cheek kids got a gunnysack full to take home. Few of the onions were wasted, and Cheek's momma had lots of ways of preparing them.

Despite the record onion crop that first year, which brought in more than $18,000 to the growers, the railroad's board of directors were slow to get the line started. The company had made ready to start the new line in 1907, but the financial panic that year created fear among the investors. Two more years went by before the line got underway. In August 1911 the first passenger train arrived in San Saba, carrying more than 1,000 people from Temple who came for the celebration. Soon the freight trains also came, hauling away pecans, wool, mohair, cattle, sheep, goats, hogs, onions, and other produce.

I don't imagine any onions are shipped out of San Saba now, but trainloads of frac sand used in oil well drilling roll through the town from Brady and tons of building materials and stone are loaded at San Saba to be marketed elsewhere. San Saba has onions to thank for bringing in its railroad.

Dead Man's Cut

Dynamite Blast Snuffs Out Lives of Two Men

THERE ARE LOTS OF INTERESTING STORIES about western Texas and the many unusual names that have been put on places and things over the years. A number of years ago the late Hallie Stillwell and her friend Virginia Madison wrote a book called *How Come It's Called That?* Their places and things were mostly located in the Big Bend Country of far West Texas.

Kathy Amos, editor of the *Eden Echo,* could perhaps put together a book of her own about the names and places that exist in Concho County, using the vast pile of information that's contained in old back issues of her newspaper, which will soon be ninety-eight years old.

Kathy gets asked frequently by readers about "such and such," and she tries to dig out the information, despite the heat or cold and the dust that accumulates in the attic. If you've ever attempted to go through stacks of old, yellowed newspapers that have been in storage for years, then you can understand how distasteful the chore can be.

While visiting with Kathy one day in her small office just off the square in Eden, we talked about how things got certain names. She related to me that a reader had inquired about how a passageway, or cut, on U.S. Highway 83 between Eden and Paint Rock got its name, "Dead Man's Cut." The rock retaining wall along the stretch of highway was being removed by Texas Department of Transportation work crews in order to be replaced with more modern retaining rails. Eden townfolks plan on using the rocks from the old retaining wall to construct bases for various new markers and entryways.

This is what she had learned about "Dead Man's Cut."

Like all country newspaper editors of long ago, J. F. Horton did not leave a morsel of information out of a news story. In those days he had plenty of space to devote to the story, particularly one of such impact as what happened at the construction site on then Texas Highway 4, about seven miles north of Eden.

"Dynamite Blast Snuffs Out Lives of Two Men," said the headline in the *Eden Echo's* front page on Thursday, August 20, 1933.

"This community was stunned this morning by a ghastly tragedy that wiped out the lives of two men in an instant. A dynamite blast, accidentally set off, hurled the bodies of Rex Lee Roggers and Richard Laman into the air and left them mere broken masses of flesh," the story stated. The accident happened a few minutes before 7 o'clock on the deep rock cut. Roggers, thirty-seven, was foreman for Baucom and Williams, contractors, and Laman, thirty-four, was helping him.

The dynamite shots, estimated at some thirteen in number, were planned for the previous day, but a rain shower had come along and caused a postponement. Apparently the damp ground caused a short in the electrical fuse setup. The men were testing the setup with a one-cell flashlight battery and flashlight bulb to determine the location of short circuits. While doing so, two dynamite shots hooked together went off beneath where the men were standing. The two shots consisted of about two cases of explosive.

> "A dynamite blast, accidentally set off, hurled the bodies of Rex Lee Roggers and Richard Laman into the air and left them mere broken masses of flesh...,"

The men were tossed high into the air. Roggers' body was hurled about 100 feet away. He was badly mangled and most all bones in his body were broken. Laman was thrown about forty feet away and was battered and broken but not as bad as Roggers.

An additional tragedy also occurred at the explosion site, Kathy said, going over the newspaper report of the accident. Roggers' wife, who had been living in Houston while he worked about the state, had arrived about 5 a.m. to visit him in Eden while she recovered from recent surgery. She had gone to the construction site with him to spend the day and had arrived only minutes before the accident. She was standing behind a power shovel when the blast occurred, only a short distance from the blast site, and saw her husband blown to bits. The couple had not seen each other since Christmas, the story stated.

The April 20 issue of the newspaper also reported that farmer Fritz Westphalen, forty-three, had been killed the day before when he was struck by a bolt of lightning, apparently during the same rainstorm that had wetted down the explosion area. Westphalen, a native of Germany, was struck at the Gromatzky farm about five miles southeast of Eden. Rudolph Schumann was nearby and was stunned by the shock.

Again, editor Horton made sure to include all the facts of the story about Westphalen.

"One odd feature of the tragedy is that this same house was struck by lightning a year ago, and while Mr. Westphalen was in bed. At the time he was shocked but not harmed. It is one instance where lightning did strike twice," the editor noted.

Another Eden resident, Mrs. A. S. Bishop, was painfully injured when she was wrenched and jostled on Monday afternoon when her coupe automobile got out of control, jumped two ditches, and hit a pole on the opposite side of the street. She was thrown against the top of the vehicle, spraining her back and sides. The car was not damaged."

"We had lots of news in those days," Kathy said.

The Bloody Salt War

Important Mineral Center of Conflict

IN FAR WEST TEXAS nearly in the shadow of El Capitan Peak is a large salt lake stretching over the plain between the Delaware and Diablo Mountains. This crystalline-impregnated mineral flat is one of the most desolate wastelands in the Southwest. Ironically, one of the bloodiest episodes in Texas history erupted over these same mineral beds.

Although called the Salt War because of the mineral beds, the fight itself happened along the Rio Grande below El Paso at San Elizaro, Ysleta, Scorro, and other communities. The Mexicans living along the river, as well as their kinsmen living on the Texas side, claimed that the lakes were of community interest and thus would be open to all comers. Large groups of folks would travel the seventy-plus miles across the sandhills and arroyos to collect the salt that crystalized along the shoreline as the lakes evaporated.

Historically, the salt lakes had been providing this important mineral to early settlers, including various Indian bands, as early as the mid-1700s. Early West Texas explorer Captain Randolph Marcy reported in one of his 1849 journals that his Mexican guide told him that his people had been using the salt for years before the Apaches stopped the salt trains. According to Marcy, the salt lay in pure state six inches thick and could be shoveled up in large quantities.

Samuel A. Maverick, a well-known Texan, emerged as the first antagonist of the river people's claim to the lakes. Maverick attained two sections of land, or 1,280 acres, in 1865 that included the choicest areas for collecting the salt. However, much of the salt-laden waters were outside of Maverick's land claims.

In order to take control over the remaining land area, a group from El Paso called the "Salt Ring," led by W. W. Mills, a local political leader, Albert J. Fountain, and Louis Cardis, was organized for the purpose of acquiring title to the salt deposits at the foot of the Guadalupes, about 100 miles east of El Paso. However, the men were to have a falling out, and Fountain would organize the "Anti-Salt Ring."

The so-called Salt Ring was an unsavory collection of characters, each trying to turn the salt deposits to his own profit. The conspiracy caught the interest of a Mexican priest, Father Antonio Barrajo. A reputed "Gringo-hater," Barrajo raced about the parish in his buggy pulled by a matched pair of high-stepping geldings. He would threaten his wards with the power of his office, thus guaranteeing the political support of his parishioners. The priest became an ally of the Salt Ring.

The various personalities involved created a bubbling brew that fermented rapidly. Political storms quickly occurred, tempers flared, and infighting began. On December 7, 1870, a Salt Ring lawyer named B. F. Williams accosted his enemy, Fountain, in Ben Dowell's Saloon. Williams emptied his derringer into the man. Luckily, Fountain did not die. But Williams raged on, shouting threats toward everyone in hearing range. When Judge Gaylord Clarke came to talk him out of the fight, Williams killed Clarke with a blast from a shotgun. Meanwhile, Fountain, still on his feet, found a rifle and shot Williams at the same time that Captain Trench of the state police fired his pistol. Williams fell dead.

This initial shooting cooled the situation somewhat until another lawyer, Charley Howard, showed up from Missouri looking for ways to enrich himself in growing El Paso. Political skullduggery followed, with Howard forming a powerful triumvirate with Louis Cardis and the Mexican priest. Cardis was elected to the Texas Legislature and subsequently helped Howard become district judge over a territory stretching over 400 miles from end to end.

As so often happens, Cardis and Howard got crossways with one another, each accusing the other of selfish motives. Meanwhile, Father Barrajo quietly moved to take sole control of the region. As a result of their falling out with each other, Howard filed on the salt lakes in the name of his father-in-law, Major George B. Zimpleman. This act outraged the Mexican citizens, who considered the salt lakes as public property under the terms of the treaty of Guadalupe Hidalgo. Cardis, who controlled the Mexican vote, and Father Barrajo supported their views.

After filing on the land, Howard struck out for Fort Quitman and the salt lakes to complete a survey of his claim. He was accompanied by a surveyor named Blanchard, a land agent named McBride, three Mexicans, and three Blacks. When stopped at San Elizaro and told to turn back, Howard and his party refused. His contempt for the border residents was his undoing.

In October 1877 a mob of Mexican-Americans took Howard prisoner near San Elizaro and forced him to sign over his claims to the salt lakes. Howard retaliated. He notified the governor that Mexican troops were going to invade the area. His former colleague, Louis Cardis, told the governor a different story. As a result, Howard sought Cardis and killed him with a shotgun. News of the slaying traveled fast. Soon, Mexicans raged against Americans. The Texas Rangers and the U.S. Army were called on for help.

The situation again cooled, but not for long. Howard and a band of followers were in San Elizaro celebrating at Charlie Ellis's store. At that moment, a mob of residents gathered to discuss ways to get rid of Howard. Ellis overheard the talk and was caught and killed as a spy. The fight was on. Howard and some twenty others, including some rangers and several soldiers, sought refuge in the rangers' quarters. Three lines of men attacked the garrison when Howard refused to surrender. The fight, which began on a Wednesday, continued until Friday. Six members of the mob were killed, and a number of others suffered wounds.

When Army Lieutenant John B. Tays discovered the Mexicans tunneling beneath the garrison, Howard was advised to give up. He signed an agreement giving up his claim to the salt lakes and turned over $11,000 in cash to the Mexicans, headed by Chico Barela.

When the priest, Father Barrajo, learned that Barela planned to release the Americans, he flew into a rage and demanded that the gringos be killed "and I will absolve you."

Being assured that they would be set free, the rangers filed out of their little fort and were disarmed and imprisoned. The mob put Howard, the land agent McBride, and another man, John G. Atkinson, before a wall, and a firing squad of Mexicans shot them to death.

A Congressional investigation was started into the affair in January 1878. There were questions why army commander Colonel Hatch had not put troops into the area quicker. Several officers resigned as a result of the inquiry. In March, when court convened, the matter was quickly dismissed. No one was punished because there were no charges brought against any of the participants in the San Elizaro violence.

One important change was made, however. Fort Bliss, which had been abandoned earlier in the year, was reestablished and has remained an active military post until the present day.

Tom Green County

IT IS HARD TO BELIEVE, but the entire Panhandle of Texas was once a part of Tom Green County because the Texas Legislature failed to give the northern boundary when the jumbo county was created in 1874.

Due to the state legislature's oversight in establishing the northern boundary of the county, sixty-six other counties would ultimately be carved from Tom Green County's original boundaries, thus making Tom Green the mother of nearly one-fourth of the state.

Tom Green County, with San Angelo as county seat, now is a mere shadow of its former self. However, the county can call itself a grandparent many times over. According to research carried out in 1934 by Judge R. C. Crane, then president of the West Texas Historical Association, the county is commonly understood to have been the mother to twelve counties located to the west. However, it is not commonly known that an additional fifty-four counties to the north also were part of the once "jumbo" Tom Green County.

These particular fifty-four counties cover an area 180 miles east and west, by 300 miles north to south, equal to the size of Kentucky, Ohio, Tennessee, Pennsylvania, New York, and Virginia. The dozen counties to the west that were carved off the jumbo county were Coke, Sterling, Glasscock, Midland, Ector, Winkler, Loving, Ward, Crane, Upton, Reagan, and Irion.

Here is how it happened that Tom Green County was originally so big.

In the days of the Texas Republic, Bexar County as it became known with San Antonio as its seat of government, comprised about one half of the republic's territory. As time passed, many counties were carved out of Bexar, including Tom Green and its vast area to the north and west. As the region drew settlers after Forts Chadbourne and Concho were established, folks wanted their own county government closer to home. It was a long way to San Antonio to conduct business, attend court, have their lands surveyed, and have deeds recorded.

As it turned out, the Texas Legislature passed a law on March 13, 1874, which provided for the creation and organization of Tom Green County. Named commissioners to organize the county were J. L. Millspaugh, G. W. Delong, W. S. Kelly, W. S. Vick, and F. C. Taylor. These men also were assigned the job of calling the election for people to vote for county officials and also select a permanent county seat.

The act passed by the state legislature called for the election to be held at Ben Ficklin on January 5, 1876. The community of Ben Ficklin was chosen the first county seat over its rival, the village of Saint Angela, located near Fort Concho, by the vote of Ficklin's Mexican employees of the stage station there. These Mexicans were recognized as naturalized citizens for the occasion of the election. However, a disastrous flood came on August 24, 1882, and destroyed the town. Subsequently, the county courthouse was relocated to San Angelo.

Eventually the legislature learned of its mistake and carved up northern portions of the huge county and attached the unorganized territory to Jack, Clay, Young, and Palo Pinto Counties for judicial, surveying, and other purposes in August 1876.

The other dozen counties were cut off of Tom Green County as each petitioned the legislature to set up their own local governments after 1884.

Although Tom Green County is no longer the granddaddy of Texas counties, it is still fairly large. According to Crane's calculations, it is still larger than the state of Rhode Island with several districts of Columbia thrown in for good measure.

2,000 Show Up for Dam Party

Rededication Fest Marks Dam's 50th Birthday

IT WAS CALLED THE "biggest dam birthday party in Texas" and I would not have missed it for a week's paycheck. Newspaper reporters don't often get a chance to party while working, and this blast at Buchanan Dam in the fall of 1987 proved to be a story long to be remembered.

About 2,000 people showed up for the celebration, including about 200 workers who literally built portions of the two-mile-long, multi-arch dam with their bare hands.

For a while that Saturday in October 1987, history threatened to repeat itself as heavy, moisture-laden skies appeared ready to dump heavy rains on the celebration. Fifty years earlier, when the dam was first dedicated in 1937, only about 500 people turned out to hear then Secretary of the Interior Harold L. Ickes praise the structure as "substantial tributes to the vigor and ability of men who conceived and brought about this project." It rained that day, too.

Ickes, a member of President Franklin D. Roosevelt's cabinet, was a noted orator, and a segment of his 1937 dedication speech was rebroadcast during the 50th anniversary party.

My trip to Buchanan Dam lasted a couple of days. Since there was no nearby motel available, I took my pop-up camping trailer and set up camp in Inks Lake State Park, a few miles away from the massive dam on the Llano-Burnet County line. There were other dam celebrants staying in the park, including a man from Houston who was camping out of his automobile in a campsite neighboring mine. He was the first professional "star-watcher" I have ever encountered. Unfortunately for him, the heavy overcast skies made watching the stars a lost cause. Thus we became friends at the campfire where we swapped stories, talking about our jobs and the birthday party.

I soon learned that the man's grandfather had helped build the dam. The man—I have forgotten his name—had grown up hearing stories about his grandpa working on the construction gangs, but he had never seen the dam. I remember well his comment that

Sunday morning when we both were packing up to go our separate ways.

"That must have been one hellva job building that dam with what tools they had then," he said, recalling his granddad talking about shoveling concrete on the project.

Buchanan Dam was named for Congressman J. P. Buchanan, who in 1934 had achieved approval from President Roosevelt for financing the dam as a Public Works Administration (PWA) project. Buchanan died in February 1937, some seven months before the dam was completed.

Special guests for the celebration were members of the "Golden Crew," construction workers who helped build the dam during the 1930s. For some of the senior citizens, most retired from years of labor, the return trip to Buchanan Dam took some time. Many lived out-of-state, coming from as far away as Oregon. Others had never moved very far away, choosing to stay in nearby towns such as Tow, Burnet, Bluffton, Llano, Marble Falls, San Saba, Kingsland, Bertrum, Austin, and other places.

The early-day builders, who with limited power equipment to help had put the concrete forms into place for the 150-foot tall dam, were given special cruises on the lake and along the dam so they could see the results of their handiwork.

A man named William Records of San Antonio told me he was among the first men on the job in 1932, the day when Fegles Construction Company of Minnesota

> "That must have been one hellva job building that dam with what tools they had then," he said,

closed down operations at 4 p.m., unable to meet the next day's payroll. Buchanan Dam was constructed intermittently between 1931 and 1937. Its origin dates from plans drawn up by General Adam R. Johnson in 1885. Johnson subsequently sold his plans to C. H. Alexander Sr., who formed the Syndicate Power Company in 1926 to build six dams on the Colorado. When construction actually started on the dam in 1931, Central Texas Hydro-Electric Company was the holder of the syndicate assets. However, when financial backers declared bankruptcy in 1932, construction was halted for four years.

The partially built dam and related assets later went into the receivership of Alvin Wirtz. A new corporation, the Colorado River Company, was formed and applied for a PWA loan of $4,500,000. The federal agency turned down the loan application primarily because the builders were a private com-

recalling his granddad talking about shoveling concrete on the project.

pany. Congressman Buchanan of Brenham persuaded President Roosevelt to approve the funds. The Lower Colorado River Authority (LCRA), patterned after the Tennessee Valley Authority, was organized when Roosevelt and the PWA required that the project be built and owned by a public agency. LCRA directors spent the first year following the organization of the agency paying off $2,630,959 to creditors from previous construction. Work then resumed on the dam on July 1, 1936.

In 1934 the Great Depression was in full swing. There were 95,442 people on relief in Central Texas. A job of any kind was a godsend. During the intermittent land clearing and construction of Buchanan, thousands of men and their families moved into the area hoping to find work. When the PWA loan was approved, officials estimated at the time that about 4,400 persons would get off the relief rolls. When the LCRA took over construction, there were 1,900 people working on the project.

Gene Mills of Austin, who worked on the dam from 1936 to 1938, remembered the long lines of job seekers that were on the job site nearly every day. "Times were tough and lots of men were out of work. The men [seeking jobs] would line up each morning. The line would be 100 yards long."

The jobs called for clearing 15,000 acres of land by hand, rock crushing, soil removal, cutting timber, carpenters, truck drivers, concrete puddlers, and general laborers. Moore Johanson of Cherokee recalls cutting trees with crosscut saws and axes. "It was the hardest work ever done in this area," he said.

Pearly Walters and her husband, Mike, of Cherokee, recalled spending their honeymoon in a tent at the Tanyard Camp. "It was tough, but I had it better than most women. We lived near the spring where we could get water and keep the milk cool," she said. The Walters married on May 22, 1937, and the dam was completed in October.

Mike Walters was foreman of a timber clearing crew and rode horseback while overseeing the work gangs. Many of the timber cutters had come from the East Texas piney woods and were experienced in handling large timber. Moore Johanson, who grew up in Lone Grove, recalled the Bluffton Valley along the Colorado River being rich farmland, with huge oak and pecan trees and lots of wildlife.

Bluffton, the hometown of Mrs. Walters, is now submerged beneath Buchanan Dam's sprawling reservoir.

"It was heartbreaking to have to give up our home, but it was worth it to get an electric iron, a refrigerator, and electric lights," she said.

Many of the workers on the dam lived in construction camps. Life wasn't easy. Some lived in tents; others lived in simple shacks put together with whatever building materials were handy.

A special meal treat came when workers in the camps were able to trap a range hog and roast it. A mess of fresh meat along with a big pan of cream gravy and hot biscuits were a real treat. The Llano-Burnet area had lots of range hogs in those days, and the landowners didn't squawk much when one was trapped and barbecued.

There was little recreation available to the workers. Those who had dependable transportation could go to Burnet, about ten to twelve miles away, and attend a movie. The families in the camps also organized baseball games, fishing parties, and held fish fries. During the afternoons, women in the camps would gather around an available radio and listen to "Ma Perkins," then a popular soap opera. Otherwise, they spent most of their time making meals, mending clothes, and carrying water from the nearest source. The campers had to haul water for all purposes.

Henry Sieber, another former worker, recalled that three shifts of men worked around the clock to complete the dam. "They had to use three shifts of workers because they couldn't shut down the [concrete] mixers," he said. Men needing work would sign up at the employment office and most would take whatever job came open. Top wage for skilled workers was $1 an hour, but the concrete workers were paid 40 cents an hour.

Among the better paid men were engineers. William Records of San Antonio, a New Yorker by birth, was a young field engineer on the construction job. He came to work on the dam in 1932 when it was still called "Hamilton Dam." He made $110 a month and had one day off a month.

According to records, the Buchanan Dam project was typical for the Depression period because there was plenty of cheap labor available. That is one reason the dam was constructed in such a manner—utilizing the multi-arch design. The multiple-arch construction was highly labor intensive but used far less concrete than any of the other dam designs for that period of time. Arches provided the most stability for the amount of concrete required, Records explained.

Lake Buchanan, formed by the dam's reservoir, is the largest in area of Texas's lakes. It measures thirty-one miles long and is up to five miles wide. The reservoir has a capacity of 992,000 acre feet and covers a surface area of 23,200 acres. An acre foot of water equals approximately 325,000 gallons.

On that special occasion in 1987, Jim Inks of Llano was on hand for the celebration. Jim Inks is the son of Roy Inks, who helped build Buchanan Dam and Inks Dam, which is downstream from the Buchanan site. Inks Dam is named for his father.

Inks recalled visiting the construction sites on many occasions. He was a fourteen-year-old schoolboy when the projects were underway. He perhaps described the occasion the best when he looked across the parking lot at the huge dam and said with a smile, "Ain't she pretty."

Rocksprings Lynching

THE 1995 MURDER of a Barksdale stockman, his wife, and hired hand on their remote ranch sounded all too familiar to my friend Dr. Gerald Raun, an Alpine writer-historian and former biology professor.

Raun, who has lived along the border country for a good number of years, got interested in a 1910 murder that nearly triggered a war between the United States and Mexico. The stories are similar because both slayings took place in the same general area of the state, and the suspect in both crimes was a Mexican national.

The November 2, 1910 slaying of Mrs. Effie Greer Henderson, the wife of Lem K. Henderson, a prominent Edwards County rancher, nearly caused an international incident between the U.S. and Mexico, which at the time was shaky due to revolutionary rhetoric that gripped the south of the border nation. It also brought about two weeks of international fame or infamy to the twenty-year-old Mexican, Antonio Rodriquez, and to the quiet ranching community of Rocksprings.

Many Texans—particularly those living in the western region of the state—are unaware that the explosive situation had the presidents of both countries talking in serious tones of ending diplomatic relations, despite neither William Howard Taft nor Porfirio Diaz knowing the location of the small Texas town.

As 1910 drew to an end, Porfirio Diaz had celebrated his eighty-third birthday and had been re-elected *presidente* of Mexico, a position that he had held for thirty-four years. On the surface, all appeared calm, but storm clouds were gathering rapidly as discontent with the Diaz regime became more intense and revolutionaries plotted against the government from safety zones north of the Rio Grande, according to secret reports from Henry Lane Wilson, then the U.S. Ambassador to Mexico, to his Washington, D.C. superiors.

Using newspaper accounts from that time and government documents from the Mexican Revolution, Raun pieced together the horrific story of the murder of Mrs. Henderson and the subsequent lynching of Rodriquez by a mob that took him from the Edwards County jail in Rocksprings and burned him at the stake. This brutal action resulted in anti-American riots in Mexico and created a serious diplomatic crisis between the two nations.

According to the book *A History of Edwards County,* published by the Rocksprings Woman's Club Historical Committee, Effie Henderson was sitting on her back porch mending clothes when a lone Mexican horseman rode up to the house and dismounted, carrying a rifle in his hand. Playing on the porch with her were two children, Hadie, six, and Lem Jr., a toddler. The man asked Mrs. Henderson where her husband was, and she told him he was at work in a pasture. When she turned away, the man shot her in the back then put a second shot into the back of her head. A Mexican woman, whose husband worked for the Hendersons, heard the shots. When the horseman left the scene, she found Mrs. Henderson's body sprawled on the porch. She quickly took the two Henderson children and her own children and hid in the brush. When her husband got home, she told him about the killing and gave a description of the Mexican rider.

L. A. Clark, a deputy sheriff and later sheriff of Edwards County, and another deputy, Perry Mayes, headed the posse that searched for the Mexican. He was found and arrested the next day on the old Hamlyn Ranch, near Rocksprings. When questioned, he admitted shooting the woman, saying that she had "spoken harshly" to him.

Rodriquez was put into jail, but about 3:30 that afternoon, November 3, 1910, a mob of about 100 men overpowered the deputies and seized the prisoner. He was taken from the jail to a location about a half-mile south of Rocksprings where he was chained to a tree and burned alive. It was a very violent and nasty death. The man's charred remains were later buried in the Rocksprings Cemetery where a small granite stone marks his grave. The inscription says: "Antonio Rodriquez, died November 3, 1910, Burned at Stake."

The lynching of Rodriquez might have been a forgotten incident were it not for the festering anti-American sentiment in Mexico and the growing opposition to the Diaz government. Soon, an inflammatory editorial appeared in a Mexico City newspaper, accusing Americans of racial hatred. Another editorial appeared several days later, calling U.S. citizens "barbarous blond men of North America," and "giants of dollars and pigmies of culture." As a result of the editorials, riots broke out. When the Mexican government was slow in putting down the protests, diplomatic ties were stretched to the breaking point.

Before the situation was brought under control, tempers were flaring up along the border and throughout northern Mexico. The big city American newspapers were covering the story closely.

As the situation appeared to calm down and investigations were being promised by both state and national officials, a report came that an armed band of Mexicans were planning to march on Rocksprings and take revenge for Rodriquez's lynching. This situation added fuel to an already overheated dispute. News reports stated that 2,000 armed cowboys had gathered at Rocksprings to defend the town. In truth, however, only about fifteen to twenty men had gathered to help the local law officers keep the peace. In addition, Governor Thomas M. Campbell had sent several Texas Rangers to check things out.

Antonio Rodriquez's name would soon disappear from the news pages, replaced by another named Francisco Madero, who issued a call for a revolution against the Diaz regime.

Although it appeared to most American diplomats that Madero was doomed to failure, a flame had been lit that would not burn out for over a decade. The atrocity of Rocksprings soon paled before the brutal reality of the civil war in Mexico where more than a million would die.

Cedar Choppers, a Vanishing Breed

Cedar Posts Became a Hot Commodity

WHATEVER HAPPENED TO THE CEDAR CHOPPERS that roamed the Texas Hill Country, whacking away at the junipers with short-handled, double-headed axes? Like the pioneer muleskinners, trappers, gunslingers, and trailblazers, these hardy outdoorsmen have about disappeared. The whacking sound of sharp cedar axes slicing into the hard wood has given way to the loud roaring of chainsaws chewing through the tough branches.

There's not much information readily available about these folks who traveled the cedar country along the Edwards Plateau region. The hills around Junction, Ingram, Camp Wood, Rocksprings, and other Hill Country communities used to be full of cedar cutters at work, but now only a few stumps remain on lands that were once clustered with junipers at times so thick a man could barely walk through them.

The cedar cutters lived a primitive existence in those hills, camping out in the breaks near where the work was being done. Some used tents; others slept under the stars or utilized some kind of small trailer as a place to seek shelter from the cold, rain, and wind.

In the early 1950s an elderly cedar chopper came to work on the McSwain farm near Brady. The man, slightly built with a head full of unruly black hair and thick beard, had suffered a severe arm injury in a cedar camp fight. He was no longer able to do a full day's work cutting cedar posts. He knew no other way of life, so he took what work he could find as a farmhand. He was a good hand, too, and a good man. Despite having little education, he had a lot of influence on my life during the short time that he lived and worked on the place because he had survived so much adversity. He seemed to know ahead of time when I was troubled, and he helped me find my way.

Names matter not as this old and respected friend is long dead, but his memory and his stories of life in the cedar camps remain vivid in my mind. My friend had spent much of his life cutting cedar around Utopia, Old

Ingram, Camp Wood, Junction, and Rocksprings. The lessons learned in those cedar breaks of poverty and even from stays in various county jails provided my friend and his companions with an education in survival. Poverty was an acceptable way of life, and money was for one thing: purchasing the necessities to sustain the body and the spirit.

Food requirements were simply staple goods—mostly coffee, flour, sugar, salt, bacon, and beans. Wild game, such as deer and turkey, taken on the place where the work was being done provided the main meat course. Food was prepared as needed, and there were no leftovers. Refrigerators don't work so well in the cedar breaks.

Clothes were mostly work shirts and blue jeans or overalls. A pair of pants and a shirt could last for quite awhile. When they got too dirty or too worn, they were simply thrown away and replaced with a new pair. There was no need for fancy clothes in the cedar breaks.

The small town of London, in Kimble County, was a favorite place for entertainment for my friend and his companions. It had a beer joint, dance hall and domino parlor, a few stores, and a post office. Saturday nights were usually pretty loud and, at times, rowdy.

With the county jail more than twenty-five miles away, folks who misbehaved usually ended up being handcuffed around a telephone pole. It was too much trouble for the deputy to take them to jail in Junction.

Cutting cedar was a dawn to

> Clothes were mostly work shirts and blue jeans or overalls. A pair of pants and a shirt could last for quite awhile. When they got too

dark occupation because a man was paid for the amount of posts and stays he cut. If a man got sick or was injured pretty badly, he stayed in camp. Otherwise, he worked if he expected to get any pay. Snakebites and other injuries were usually taken care of using home remedies. Doctors didn't make calls in the cedar breaks.

I lost track of my old friend, the cedar cutter, and learned of his death a number of years later when I saw his death notice in the local paper. My friend had died after being sick for a long time, a family member told me later. I have often wondered how he got along during those final days, pampered by nurses and stretched out in a clean, soft bed. Pampering women and clean sheets were something he never experienced in the cedar breaks.

A few months after publishing my column on cedar whackers, my mailbox was full of recollections

dirty or too worn, they were simply thrown away and replaced with a new pair. There was no need for fancy clothes in the cedar breaks.

about cedar choppers. Perhaps the most interesting letter came from A. Lafayette "Red" Cheek of Stillwater, Oklahoma, who wrote to tell me that his family spent a lot of time in the cedar breaks around San Saba when he was a boy.

Cheek described his age as "smooth-mouth," his weight "too much," and an "unknown amount of mileage" on his hide. He said he was a "has been" teacher, coach, marine, musician, horse wrangler, and a genuine fugitive from the

Grapes of Wrath.

According to Cheek's letter, his mother and father married in 1912 and moved to the Scholten cedar break near Bend in San Saba County.

"Cedar posts had become a hot commodity with the perfection of barbed wire. So much so that a railroad was built from Lometa, in Lampasas County, south across the Colorado River down near Gorman Falls," Cheek wrote.

According to the *San Saba County History Book, 1856-1983*, cedar was developing into big business in the southeastern part of San Saba County in the early 1900s, and it continued to be an economic factor until the 1950s. In those early days heart cedar was cut and hauled by wagon and teams from cedar camps to various cedar yards on a year-round basis.

The potential to make some big money depended on getting the cedar posts and fencing stays to western markets. A number of investors saw this potential, including members of the Dutch royal family. In 1910 two enterprising engineers, Edward and Alfred Scholten, arrived in Lometa and set about constructing a narrow-gauge railroad from the Santa Fe Railroad yards there to the Heller cedar break located on the Lemons Ranch some twenty-five to thirty miles away. It took two years to build the short line, but once completed two trains of eight cars each started moving cedar posts and stays. The locomotives got their water from Gorman Springs. The rail line crossed the Colorado River just below Cowell Crossing. However, the unpredictable river washed the bridge out three times before 1918.

"Scholtens ran their own commissary in a large tent," Cheek recalled. "One night during a very violent windstorm, almost everybody's tent blew away so almost the entire village slept in the commissary. I don't know how long the Scholten cedar break lasted, but they were still in business when my older brother and sister were born in April 1914.

"In 1927 my older brother, now thirteen, would stay out of school a few days, cut a wagonload of cedar posts, and take them into Bend to trade for groceries. As a six-year-old, I tagged along with him, but I never knew what he was paid for the posts," Cheek wrote.

Cheek said he quickly learned then, and later during the Great Depression, that cutting cedar was a "last resort" as a way to make money.

"During the summer of 1934 there was no work, and I suggested to my father we cut a load of posts like my older brother had done at Bend back in '27. He insisted there was no market, but my brother, Joe, and I decided to cut a load anyway. In a few days the two of us had forty-eight regular posts 5½ feet long and 3½ inches in diameter, and two big posts, 8 feet long by 4½ inches. We stacked them and quit. Lo and behold, a couple of weeks later a rancher from over in Llano County came and bought all we had. He paid a nickel for each of the forty-eight regular posts and a dime each for the big posts. That $2.60 was enough to buy almost a week's worth of groceries," Cheek recalled.

C. W. Wimberley in Houston also wrote concerning the cedar cutters. He noted that cedar choppers were among the last of the truly independent American craftsmen, and cutting posts was their trade.

"The cedar cutter possessed a special skill with the axe which he used to turn cedar timber into the most marketable kind of post. In a five-to-six-hour day, he could cut nearly 100 clean posts if he was working in a fair stand of cedar," Wimberley observed.

Frederica Wyatt of Junction reminded me that cutting cedar could be hazardous to your health during the pioneer days. A young frontiersman, James Sewell, was murdered by Indians in 1872 while cutting cedar in the Bear Creek wilderness.

The late Congressman O. Clark Fisher, who retired to his Angora goat ranch near Junction after spending several decades in Congress, reported in one of his history papers that President Franklin D. Roosevelt's administration had offered various agriculture subsidies to ranchers in the 1930s to encourage range management programs, one of which was a cedar eradication program. Ironically, the pesky mountain juniper became an economic blessing in disguise to Kimble County folks with the establishment of a large cedar mill and special plant where cedar wood products are manufactured, along with the extraction of cedar oil.

"The lowly cedar tree still provides a living for many Kimble County residents," Mrs. Wyatt said.

The Violent World of the Frontier

Living History Groups Bring the Past to Life

THE MUSKETS ROARED and belched clouds of white smoke. Quickly, the soldiers went through the motions of reloading their rifles and making ready for another salvo. The war was on, but no bullets were zipping through the air to cause ghastly wounds in the ranks of warriors.

For scores of youngsters, seeing a battle reenactment where the sounds are real, the smoke burns the eyes, and people shout commands over the noise, history takes on a new meaning. One of the more popular activities during warm weather now is historic reenactments of various events from the frontier days. Several times during the year, groups of reenactors from all over the state gather at different locations to put on a show. Among the more popular places are the Alamo in downtown San Antonio, old Fort Martin Scott at Fredericksburg, Fort McKavett near Menard, Fort Lancaster near Sheffield in far West Texas, and at Fort Davis.

While the most thrilling event for youngsters is the weapons demonstrations where blanks are fired and horses gallop about the parade grounds, grownups get a chance to look over and handle various artifacts that generally are on display.

As one reenactor said, "it's a new way to study history."

At a recent "Fall of the Alamo" presentation, more than 150 living history participants took part, demonstrating all kinds of frontier activities.

"Ninety-nine percent of the time there weren't any battles, just surviving frontier life," said Bob Benavides, chairman of the San Antonio Living History Association. The number one goal of his organization is to correct misconceptions about prairie life.

While reenactors in the immediate San Antonio area take pride in telling the story of the Alamo, others focus on different periods of life on the frontier. Of special interest is the Buffalo Soldiers, units composed of African-Americans who served on the western frontier after the Civil War.

Buffalo Soldiers was the name given to members of four regiments by the Plains Indians, particularly to two cavalry regiments of African-Americans that

served on the frontier in the post-Civil War army. More than 180,000 black soldiers had seen service in segregated units in the Union army. Many of these units achieved outstanding combat records.

In 1866, when the Congress reorganized the peacetime army, it recognized the merits of black soldiers, thus it established two regiments of cavalry—the 9th and the 10th—and six regiments of black infantry. In 1869, however, the black infantry regiments were consolidated into two units: the 24th and the 25th Infantry.

From 1866 to the early 1890s, these soldiers served at many Texas posts, in the southwestern section of the country, and on the Great Plains. They were the backbone of the frontier army charged with protecting settlers from bands of hostile Indians, such as the Comanche, Apache, Kiowa, Cheyenne, Sioux, and the Arapaho.

During the Indian War period, thirteen enlisted men from the

Above: *Frontier reenactor and his riding mule at Fort McKavett, Texas. Ross McSwain collection.*

inception. The regiment was barely two months old when a recruiting party came to Lake Providence, in East Carroll Parish, north of Vicksburg in the Mississippi Delta country. Stance was then nineteen years old and stood just five feet tall. He enlisted in F Troop and joined the regiment in New Orleans, and after training for a couple of months, he and other recruits boarded trains for San Antonio. In June 1867 Stance and his troop were assigned to Fort Davis, in far West Texas.

According to Army records, Stance endured nine years of hard campaigning in Texas. During this time he was promoted to sergeant. Also during this time he won his Medal of Honor.

On the morning of May 20, 1870, Stance was in command of a small detachment of soldiers on a scout north from Fort McKavett, in Menard County, a post located some 150 miles from San Antonio. The detachment came on a party

four regiments earned the Medal of Honor for heroic actions against the hostiles. Among these winners were several Seminole Indian scouts and a feisty Sergeant Emanuel Stance, a tough, wiry Louisianan who had been with the 9th Cavalry since nearly its of Kickapoo Indians with a horse herd. The soldiers drove away the warriors, rounded up the horses, and camped for the night at Kickapoo Springs. The next morning, while en route to the fort, Stance and his troopers came upon another band of Indians and were able to capture more horses. However, the Indians wanted them back so they attacked the patrol—not once but twice. In the rapidly moving fight, Stance and the troopers came upon the Indian camp and rescued two white prisoners.

As a result of these skirmishes and the rescue of the white prisoners from the Indians, Stance was awarded the Medal of Honor at Fort McKavett on July 20, 1870. He was the first black trooper to be awarded the medal for heroism against an Indian enemy. He stayed at Fort McKavett for three additional years and later served with General Ranald S. Mackenzie's campaign against the Comanches and Kiowa in 1874.

A little-known band of Texans —descendants of fugitive Negro slaves that intermarried with Florida Seminole Indians during the 1820s—played a major role in ridding frontier Texas of hostile Indians during the Indian Wars of the nineteenth century.

These people, carrying the family names of Factor, July, Fay, Payne, Warrior, Bowlegs, and others, served as Seminole Indian scouts. Many of their lineage still live in Brackettville, a small southwest Texas community between Uvalde and Del Rio. The village grew in the shadow of Fort Clark, once a premier frontier station for many legendary cavalrymen.

In the 1820s and 1830s many runaway slaves from Georgia and the Carolinas took refuge among the Florida Seminoles, where they learned to hunt, trail, and fight. During the Seminole Indian War that ended in 1835, the Negro-Seminoles served as guides, interpreters, and warriors against the United States. As a result of their hostile activities, they were relocated to Indian Territory, now Oklahoma, but even there they were harassed by slave owners and other Indians. To escape this persecution, Chief John Horse led a large band of Negro-Seminoles into Mexico in 1848, settling in the vicinity of Nacimiento. The Negro-Seminoles formed an excellent barrier between the

Mexicans and the raiding Comanches, thus the Negro-Seminoles were given provisions, equipment, and land to farm. The Negro-Seminole chief, John Horse, called Juan Caballo by the Mexicans, proved to be a fearsome leader, and the Mexicans respected him.

In 1870, weary of the raiding, murder, and other crimes committed by the hostile Indians on the U.S. side of the Rio Grande, cavalry captain Frank W. Perry was sent into Mexico to contact Negro-Seminoles and persuade them to return to U.S. soil and serve as scouts for the army. Under terms of a treaty, the U.S. government would pay the expenses of their return to Texas, grant them pay, provide them with provisions for their families, and give them grants of land for their services.

Most of the Seminole Indian scouts were assigned duty at Fort Clark. Others were assigned duty at Fort Duncan, near present-day Eagle Pass. They were to serve in this general area for twenty-five years in support of various cavalry units that were assigned patrol duty along the Texas-Mexico border. Most of the time, the scouts were under the command of a fiery, red-faced lieutenant named John Bullis. Bullis was later to gain fame and fortune during his service on the Texas frontier and eventually become a brigadier general.

In a dozen actions over an eight-year period, the Negro-Seminole Indian scouts fought side by side with the cavalrymen. They fought in Mexico as well as across the endless stretches of West Texas desert, into New Mexico and the Texas Panhandle. None were killed or even seriously wounded in all these many scraps with the Indians.

The Negro-Seminole Indian scouts formed a unique and effective fighting force. They never numbered more than fifty to sixty men. Noted historian Robert M. Utley, an authority on post-Civil War Indian-fighting activity, notes that the scouts were "perhaps the most consistently effective Indian auxiliaries the army employed."

In the spring of 1875, Bullis and a small detachment of scouts barely escaped with their lives after attacking a large force of Comanche raiders on the Pecos River, more than 100 miles from Fort Clark, their base headquarters. Three scouts accompanied

Above: *Company of Buffalo Soldiers in full dress uniform at Fort Davis, circa 1886. Photo courtesy* San Angelo Standard-Times.

Bullis that fateful day: Private Pompey Factor, Trumpeter Isaac Payne, and Sergeant John Ward.

At Eagle's Nest crossing on the Pecos River, somewhat north of present-day Langtry, Bullis and the three scouts came upon a band of twenty-five to thirty Indians driving a large herd of stolen horses across the river. Dismounting and hiding in the brush, Bullis and his men crept up on the Indians to within seventy-five yards then opened fire on the unsuspecting warriors. During the firefight, Bullis and the three scouts were able to recapture the horse herd but later lost them

when the Indians counterattacked the troopers.

Armed with army issue Sharps carbines, Bullis and his companions found themselves being encircled. The Indians could tell where the troopers were hiding from the puffs of white smoke created by the rifles' black powder loads. The men quickly returned to their horses and mounted in order to get away from the Indians. The scouts were in the saddle quickly, but Bullis's frightened horse was uncontrollable, and the officer lost the animal. Sergeant Ward, seeing that Bullis was not behind him in the retreat, turned his horse around and rushed to Bullis's aid. With Payne and Factor alongside keeping up a steady covering fire, Ward scooped Bullis up behind him and carried him to safety.

In his report later, Bullis noted that he had lost his horse and saddle, but that Ward had "just saved my hair."

In eleven days Bullis and his three troopers had covered more than 325 miles, fought an overwhelming force, killed three Indians, and wounded a number of others. On May 28, 1875, the U.S. Congress agreed with Bullis's report that the scouts "deserved a medal." The three Seminole Indian scouts were each awarded the Medal of Honor.

As the Indian Wars drew to a close in the early 1890s, the scouts were disbanded by the Army. Many remained in the Fort Clark area and in Brackettville, becoming cowboys on area ranches, horse trainers, laborers, and sheepherders. When they died, the scouts were buried in the small cemetery near the fort, along with many of their descendants. Four of the scouts were awarded Medals of Honor. Pompey Factor and John Ward are buried in different sections of the cemetery. Isaac Payne, the trumpeter, is buried beside Adam Paine, a private. The two men are not related, but they sleep eternally side by side.

Left: *Buffalo Soldiers at camp in the field, circa 1890. Photo courtesy* San Angelo Standard-Times.

The "Hoodoo" War

MASON COUNTY DEPUTY SHERIFF John Wohrle was helping his friend, a man named Harcourt, and a hired hand dig a water well on the west side of town. The day was extra hot, as most August days are in the Texas Hill Country. A young man rode up to the well on this particular day in 1875 and struck up a conversation with Wohrle.

The rider was pleasant and casually asked the deputy if he had a strip of leather he might give him to tie his rifle to his saddle. Wohrle, known to be the neighborly sort, gave the young man a strip of leather, then turned away to help the hired hand pull Harcourt from the well. It was the last thing he would ever do for a stranger.

The men had started tugging the rope to pull Harcourt up when the shot rang out. Wohrle pitched forward as the bullet tore through his brain. The hired hand scrambled to hide in a nearby brush pile. Harcourt hollered as the rope gave way, and he plunged into the unfinished well where he was knocked unconscious.

The horseman dismounted, fired five more bullets into Wohrle's body, then scalped him. Scott Cooley had avenged the death of one of his friends, Tim Williamson.

Wohrle's death was just one of many bloody episodes that took place in Mason County during the 1870s, most of which were attributed to the Hoodoo War.

The late Margaret Bierschwale, a native of Mason County and longtime educator, said the ill-fated years after the Civil War laid the foundation for the Mason County War, which started with disturbances in 1869, followed by several incidents in 1873 and 1874. Cattle thieves were running rampant across the state, and Mason County was on the threshold of starting its own cattle industry, thus rustlers were busy in western Texas as well. There were too many bands of thieves and too few law enforcement officers, she would later write in a comprehensive history of her county.

There also were other reasons behind the bloodshed. There still existed much ill feeling between the American and German settlers. Many of the Germans, who had immigrated to the United States from Germany prior to the Civil War, were Union sympathizers. On the other hand, many of the Americans had been supporters and soldiers for the Confederacy, thus an unspoken feud between them was the result. Neighbors were no longer "real neighborly" as in the past.

Members of the Hoodoo mob could not have imagined what kind of trouble they would bring to the community as a result of their efforts to stop the cattle thieves. Anglo ranchers started carrying weapons, and talk was rampant that the Anglos would take revenge upon the "Dutchmen." As a result of the rumors, the German settlers started sticking together, traveling only in groups, and became suspicious of anyone coming near their homes.

Although there were disagreements and other problems, it was murder committed by both factions that aggravated the affair.

On February 13, 1875, Mason County Sheriff John Clark arrested nine men for stealing cattle. During the following week, one of the men was bound over to the grand jury and placed under a $5,000 bond. The man was said to be the ringleader of the rustlers.

On February 17 a dead man was found with a "card on his breast" saying he would not stop stealing cattle so he was killed. The slaying took the situation out of the hands of county officers, and bloodshed was soon to follow.

That night, residents near the jail were awakened by a loud commotion. A mob had formed, and they were taking the cattle thieves out of the jail. Sheriff Clark and several others had gone to the jail to investigate the situation. The sheriff attempted to stop the mob's entry into the jail. When he locked the door and rushed away to seek help, the mob battered the door open and took the men by force.

The accused rustlers, led by brothers Pete and Lige Baccus, were taken out on the Fredericksburg road, apparently to meet their fate at the end of a rope.

The sheriff, accompanied by Texas Ranger Captain Dan Roberts and several others, followed. Only the sheriff was on horseback; the others were on foot. When several shots were fired in their general direction, the small posse returned fire. When the sheriff and ranger captain arrived in a grove of oaks, the Baccus brothers were dangling from a tree limb along with their confederates, Tom Turley and Abe Wiggins. The Baccus brothers were dead, but both Turley and Wiggins were still alive. Wiggins had been shot in the head. A fifth man, Charlie Johnson, had escaped the mob by fleeing into the brush.

The bodies of the dead and near dead were brought back to Mason in a wagon. Wiggins, with most of his head blown away, died in the early morning. Turley, who nearly strangled to death at the end of a rope, recovered and was returned to jail. Unknown to the sheriff, the ranger, and local citizens, a reign of terror was starting to grip Mason County.

Ironically, a few weeks later a man named Caleb Hall, who had been a member of the posse headed by Sheriff Clark to catch the cow thieves, was arrested and put in jail with Turley for allegedly stealing cattle. Tom Gamel, another member of the posse, was singled out as one of the men who voiced opposition to the hanging of the Baccus brothers and others. Soon, rumors were spreading about the town that Turley, Hall, and Gamel would be the next guests at a "necktie party." The men took the rumor seriously and made plans. Turley and Hall escaped jail one night and fled the county. Gamel gathered some thirty armed stockmen from the surrounding area and rode into Mason to confront the sheriff and the mob's secret membership. As the Gamel crowd rode into Mason from one direction, Clark and others quickly rode out the other end of town. Gamel and his thirty riders controlled the town for two days then left and returned home.

By mid-March of 1875, Mason County residents were nervous, afraid, and concerned about their families and their futures. When Sheriff Clark returned to Mason on March 24 at the head of a band of sixty armed men, all Germans, it appeared that the Anglos and the German population would soon be involved in a bitter and bloody fight. Gamel gathered his forces again and rode into town, where the two groups of men met on the courthouse square. It was a very tense moment until the men started talking with each other then stacked their arms. A truce was made provided that mob justice would end and lawmen were allowed to start doing their jobs.

Some believe the truce might have lasted if old quarrels and disagreements had not resurfaced.

A few weeks before the Baccus gang was lynched, a popular thirty-three-year-old cowboy named Tim Williamson had been arrested for having a stolen yearling in his possession. Williamson was employed by one of the largest ranchers in the area, Carl Lehmberg of Castell in neighboring Llano County. Lehmberg, himself a German, had made a deal with Williamson to pay him $5 per head for every stray calf he brought in to the ranch. This arrangement did not sit well with some of the people, and tempers again were strained.

When Williamson was arrested, another prominent German, Dan Hoerster, posted his bond, and Williamson was released.

To make matters worse, Sheriff Clark, also serving as county tax assessor-collector, had overvalued Williamson's home in Loyal Valley, located between Mason and Fredericksburg. Clark paid a visit to Williamson's home to confront him about unpaid taxes, but he was away. Clark reportedly unleashed a tirade of abuse on Williamson's wife. When the cowboy learned of this, he rode into Mason and challenged Sheriff Clark to a "man-to-man fight." The sheriff refused. This particular incident would set the stage for the next bloody act.

Deputy John Wohrle was sent to the Lehmberg ranch on the morning of May 13 to inform Williamson that his bond had been withdrawn. He was to accompany Wohrle to Mason and be held until a new bond could be posted. Williamson's employer, Lehmberg, offered to post the bond, but he was told that he would have to go into Mason to do it. The men set out with Wohrle. Williamson was disarmed before the trip, and Wohrle made the cowboy ride his old horse while he took Williamson's young pony.

The three men had traveled about ten miles when they were stopped by a group of armed, masked men. Wohrle and Lehmberg quickly spurred their horses up the road, but Williamson's old horse could not keep up. The group of men opened fire, hitting Williamson's horse. In the next few minutes, Williamson was hit by a barrage of bullets. Reportedly, before he was killed Williamson recognized one of the masked men, Peter Bader, a German farmer. He pleaded for his life, but Bader ignored him, saying that Williamson was a rustler and needed to die. Supposedly, Bader fired the fatal shot that killed Williamson.

There quickly was talk about revenge among the American stockmen, and the first revenge killings soon began. Three Germans, Henry Doell, August Keller, and Fritz Kothmann, were camped near Willow Creek. It was a hot July night so the men did not have a very large campfire going. By surprise, bullets zinged into the camp, hitting Keller in the foot and Doell in the stomach. Kothmann was not hit in the surprise attack, but Doell died several days later. The attack was first attributed to Indians, but no Indian sign could be found. Rather, some cigarette butts were found near the site of the attack, along with spent bullet casings.

A Mason County grand jury started investigating the shootings but was having little success in developing information. Charlie Johnson, the man who had escaped the lynch mob when the Baccus brothers were hanged, was brought in and questioned about the identity of mob members. He remained silent, apparently recognizing some faces looking at him from the jury box.

Meanwhile, a young cowboy appeared in Mason and expressed interest in learning about Tim Williamson's death. There were rumors that some of Williamson's friends had sworn revenge. This young man, Scott Cooley, was a Williamson friend. In fact, Cooley had lived for a while in the Williamson home after his parents had been killed and scalped by Indians. He had been taken captive by the Indians and had spent time in their camp before escaping. Later, he joined the Frontier Battalion of the Texas Rangers.

The first man Cooley went after was Deputy Wohrle, who he gunned down and scalped on August 10, 1875. Other killings would follow.

The feud became more intense when Cooley gathered some of his pals to help him. Among these friends were known outlaws George Gladden, brothers John and Mose Beard of Blanco, and a man named

John Reingold, alias Johnny Ringo. The group made their headquarters at Gladden's farm at Loyal Valley.

According to some, Cooley was never the same man after the slaying of Wohrle. He hid his eyes beneath the brim of his hat, paid little attention to people, and refused to shake hands with anyone, preferring to keep his gun hand free at all times.

Cooley's gang terrorized the German settlers in the Loyal Valley area, including John Meusebach, the dignified old German statesman and once member of German royalty who helped settle Fredericksburg. However, his next target was Carl Bader, the brother of Peter Bader who had killed Williamson while the man begged for his life.

On August 18, 1875, Bader was working in a field on his Llano County farm when Cooley and Ringo approached. Before Bader could flee, he was gunned down.

News of Bader's death spread quickly. Sheriff Clark, who had become the head of the German element, hired a local gambler named Jim Cheney to go to Loyal Valley and make contact with Cooley and his bunch and convince them to come into Mason. George Gladden and Mose Beard agreed. As the pair approached Keller's Store on the Llano River just east of Mason, they saw Sheriff Clark standing on the porch. As the men determined what to do, a volley of shots came from behind a stone fence. Both men were seriously wounded but succeeded in riding about a mile to Beaver Creek with the sheriff's posse in hot pursuit. Mose Beard died by the creek from his wounds. Gladden, too badly wounded to fight, surrendered. Peter Bader, among the posse men, wanted to finish off Gladden but was deterred by John Keller, who swore he would kill the first man to shoot the wounded man. According to one account of the fight, Bader satisfied his vengeance by taking Mose Beard's gold ring, finger and all.

The situation in Mason County was getting intolerable. A petition was circulated and sent to Governor Richard Coke for help. On September 21, 1875, after John Beard had buried his brother, Mose, he returned to Mason County, and the festering feud became an all-out war.

Major John B. Jones, commander of the frontier ranger battalion, who had been in neighboring Menard County chasing thieves, quickly arrived with a detachment of men. As soon as the rangers arrived, the bloodshed got worse.

About September 24 Cooley's gang slipped into Mason again with Gladden along having recovered from his wounds suffered at the Keller Store ambush. Meanwhile, Ringo and another man named Williams rode to gambler Jim Cheney's home on Comanche Creek where they found him getting ready to eat breakfast. Cheney, concerned about whether the men knew of his involvement in the Keller Store shooting, tried to keep his eye on them. While he washed then dried with a towel, Ringo quietly drew his pistol and shot Cheney off the porch. The man's family watched horrified from inside the house.

After the Cheney killing, Ringo and his companion, Williams, rode into Mason and joined Cooley, Gladden, and several others at the Bridges Hotel where they ate breakfast together. Ringo reportedly was overheard boasting that "he had made beef of Cheney and if somebody didn't go bury him soon, he would start to stink."

Cooley and his band remained in town for "quite some time" and were never bothered by citizens or anyone else. The sheriff was holed up at Keller's Store with a large band of men, but there was no law in Mason.

Ranger Jones noted that when he arrived in Mason on September 28, 1875, the town was quiet "as death." The town was closed, and the few people he was able to question could not tell him anything of value to his investigation. Perhaps unknown to Jones, Cooley and his men were watching him from Gamel's Saloon.

On September 29, 1875, County Brand Inspector Dan Hoerster rode down Mason's main street accompanied by his brother-in-law, Peter Jordan, and Henry Pluenneke. The three men were well-known and prominent Germans. The trio stopped to converse with storekeeper David Doole, an Irish merchant who was friendly with most of the Germans in the area. Perhaps Doole told Hoerster and his companions that Cooley and his gang were in town. If Doole had warned the men, they apparently were not intimidated.

As the men rode away from Doole's store and upon reaching the Southern Hotel, they were fired upon by several men hiding inside a barbershop across from the hotel. Hoerster was hit in the neck by a shotgun blast, knocking him from his horse. The shot caused Jordan's young horse to rear up, making him a hard target to hit. As other shots followed, Jordan and Pluenneke hit the ground and returned fire. Hotel guests, caught in the crossfire, scrambled to safety behind whatever protection they could find. Several people in the hotel suffered gunshot wounds.

When the gunfire ended, Jordan and Pluenneke went to the wounded Hoerster. They found the brand inspector dead. Jordan had been grazed by a bullet that left a deep slash wound above his left eye. The men took Hoerster's body to the hotel. Meanwhile, Cooley and his men went to the Gamel Saloon, had a drink, then mounted up and headed out of town. As they galloped past the hotel, Jordan fired several shots at the men and hit Gladden in the hand.

Things were in a mess when Major Jones arrived in Mason that afternoon from Keller's Store on the Llano. The ranger commander sent three detachments out to search for the Cooley gang, but he reported there was little hope they would find anyone.

"They know the country well and have many friends in this and other counties," Major Jones reported to the adjutant general. "The National prejudice is very bitter here. American against German . . . I find it impossible to get a consistent or reliable account of the troubles," he wrote.

The Mason County affair was now getting attention statewide. Correspondents from various state newspapers were writing about the killings and noting that neighbors were afraid of each other and people traveled only in groups.

"Apprehension is that the worst has not yet come," one reporter stated.

Major Jones found that he had troubles in the ranks of his ranger detachments. Day after day the rangers would go out seeking Cooley and his followers but return empty-handed. It quickly became apparent to Jones that many of his men were friends of Cooley from his days in the Texas Rangers. Also, some of the rangers were more sympathetic to the Americans than to the Germans. In frustration, Jones assembled his company of rangers and told them that if any could not pursue Cooley for any reason, he would grant them an honorable discharge. Seven men stepped out, with three taking discharges. Jones quickly brought in another company of rangers from another area of the frontier where the men would not have known Cooley or any of his cohorts.

By December it seemed to Jones that Cooley was invincible to being caught. But he was elated to learn before Christmas that Cooley and one of his companions, John "Johnny Ringo" Reingold, had been arrested and jailed in Burnet County by Sheriff A. J. Strickland. When the Burnet sheriff learned that some of Cooley's friends planned to break him out of jail, he sent the prisoners to Austin for safekeeping. Unfortunately, the two outlaws were treated as celebrities.

With Cooley and Ringo locked up, Ranger Jones assumed that the Mason County troubles were about over. He was wrong. There would be one more killing.

Peter Bader, who had killed Williamson earlier in the year while he was being escorted to Mason to make a new bond, had been hiding out on San Fernando Creek in Llano County. George Gladden and John Beard were still looking for him. When they found out where he was, the two men set an ambush for him on the road between Castell and Llano. As Bader passed a granite outcropping, Beard got his revenge for Bader killing his brother, Mose. Later Beard showed the gold ring that Bader had cut from his brother's hand.

"Bader cut off my brother's finger to get his ring, and I cut Pete's finger off to get it back," Beard bragged.

Sheriff Clark, who had attempted to lead the German faction in the war, had been indicted for taking part in the disappearance of a prisoner, Bill Coke, who had been involved in the Hoerster ambush in Mason. When the charges were dropped against him, Clark resigned and fled the county. He heard that Cooley and Ringo had sworn to kill him.

The Hoodoo War actually came to an end in the fall of 1876 when gunman Scott Cooley fell gravely ill. He had eaten dinner at the Nimitz Hotel in Fredericksburg when he became sick. It was believed he had been poisoned by sympathetic Germans. However, it was more likely that he had been seized by "brain fever," which he had suffered from youth. He died and was buried in Blanco County.

The others in Cooley's gang also drifted away from the Mason area. John Beard would be heard from again several years later when he got involved in the Lincoln County War in New Mexico where he was among those shot to death. Johnny Ringo and George Gladden were captured at the Mosely Ranch near Castell in Llano County in November 1876. Gladden was the only person to stand trail for his crimes. He was convicted of murdering Peter Bader and given a 99-year sentence in the state prison. He was pardoned in 1884 and left the state.

Johnny Ringo was held in jail until 1878 charged with the murder of Jim Cheney, the Mason gambler. He was eventually acquitted and left Texas for Arizona where he got into trouble with the Earp brothers at Tombstone. He was found dead in a canyon propped against a tree with a bullet wound in his head. Some say he was killed by Buckskin Frank Leslie, a noted pistolero at the time. Others say Doc Holliday killed him. Other evidence shows he killed himself. He was the last of the Hoodoo bunch to die.

Some forty years after the Mason County War was over, a former Texas Ranger named Norman Rodgers finally broke a promise of secrecy of a meeting between himself and Scott Cooley that had been written down in Major Jones's records.

Soon after Cooley had killed John Wohrle at the well, Rodgers got permission from Captain Dan Roberts to ride over to Joe Frank's cow outfit to exchange his horse for a better one. When Rodgers rode into the cowboy camp, he noticed a man resting under a tree near the campfire. The stranger called one of the cowboys and asked him who the rider was. As Rodgers left camp the man followed him and asked if he knew Major Reynolds of the Texas Rangers. Rodgers said he knew Reynolds very well.

The man declared that he was Scott Cooley and reached into his pocket and pulled out John Wohrle's scalp. "You take this to Major Reynolds with my compliments, but don't you tell anyone you saw me," Cooley said.

No doubt there are other secrets yet to be revealed about the Mason County Hoodoo War, but they are deeply buried and will probably stay that way along with the bones of the missing men, like those of Bill Coke and a few others.

The Menard Stink House

Trapping Flies to Help Fight Screwworms

IN 1929, APPROXIMATELY forty years before scientists were able to figure out how to eradicate the costly screwworm fly, the Bureau of Entomology and Plant Quarantine established a small research laboratory at Menard. Its goal: develop a wound protectant that would be the first truly effective medicine for wormy animals. Few realized then that this early work would result in the eradication of the screwworm fly from the North American continent and most of South America as well and save the American livestock industry hundreds of millions of dollars.

Screwworms and blowflies have always been a major problem for the livestock industry, particularly sheep and goat ranchers. There were such heavy losses of livestock to the pests right after the turn of the century that ranchers started seeking help from the U.S. government as early as 1913.

Screwworms, the larvae of a certain kind of fly, called the *Cochliomyia Americana*, develop as the fly's eggs hatch deep in a wound on an animal. These wounds could be from accidental causes, such as cuts, broken horns, or from animals fighting during breeding time, or from man-made wounds, such as dehorning or castration. As the eggs develop into the larvae, or worms, inside the wound, rapid infections develop, and the animal quickly loses weight and appetite and dies. The worms have a screw-like appearance, which allows them to burrow deep into a wound, thus the name.

As a result of screwworms, ranches had to employ large numbers of cowboys to ride the range, seek out the "wormy" animals, rope them, and then treat them with some sort of homemade medicine, usually a mixture containing kerosene or other oily substance. At the ranchers' request for government assistance, two medical entomologists and a biochemist came to West Texas to study the situation and make some recommendations. According to these early studies, the researchers found that the flies could be controlled by using meat-baited fly traps and burning the carcasses of dead animals found on the range. They also recommended that ranchers stop doing procedures that made wounds on their animals during the period when the flies were most prevalent. Where screwworms were found, the scientists suggested using pine tar oil on the wound to repel the flies, and if maggots were found, they recommended that benzole be applied to kill the larvae.

When the recommendations were released by the Department of Agriculture, county agents around the Southwest began educating ranchers to use the medications and refrain from dehorning, docking, or otherwise causing wounds during warm weather.

Walker Nesbit, the Menard County extension agent, was among those early officials to tell ranchers about the screwworm menace and attempt to do something about it through trapping flies all over the county. In 1932 ranchers using traps designed by the researchers caught 33,508 quarts of flies during a period from March 1 to the end of October. A photograph of the trapped flies showed a pile of the pests fifteen feet wide and about ten feet tall. From a distance the pile looked like a pyramid of dark-colored sand.

A small laboratory, established in Menard County by the Bureau of Entomology and Plant Quarantine, was located in the back room of Emory C. Cushing's home in 1929. Later the lab was moved to another location and eventually was situated on a place about three miles west of Menard on the Dan Crowell Ranch on the old Fort McKavett Road. Here, scientists Roy Melvin, H. E. Parish, R. C. Bushland, and E. F. Knipling initiated the first real research on eradicating the screwworm fly. The lab building, about twelve by thirty feet, consisted of two narrow rooms. One room was used to raise flies and the other was used to test insecticides and other materials used to kill the flies. The worms were raised in No. 3 washtubs containing some 3½ gallons of very smelly meat slurry, thus Menard folks gave the place its name, "the stink house."

It was in this odoriferous location that the scientists first developed an improved remedy for wormy animals in 1941. The remedy, called Smear 62, became an effective killer of deeply burrowed worms, was quick in its treatment, and also provided protection against reinfestation. The black, smelly concoction got its name because it was the 62nd in a series of several hundred formulations.

The outbreak of World War II and subsequent years limited work on eradicating the screwworm fly. However, of greater interest today is the work done at the small lab. While developing medicinals like Smear 62 and later, EQ 335, the scientists also learned other things about the flies. While observing the mating behavior of trapped flies in 1937, Dr. Knipling determined that the female screwworm fly was monogamous. After mating once, the female fly rejected all other males. Knipling assumed that if all male flies could be sterilized, an entire population of screwworm flies could be eradicated.

These early observations and tests in the Menard Stink House would eventually lead to the creation of the International Screwworm Eradication Program many years later, which has saved the livestock industry hundreds of millions of dollars from lost animals, reduced the need for ranch labor, and reduced or completely eliminated the need for ranchers to buy costly medications.

Bibliography

American Folklore and Legend. The Reader's Digest Association, Pleasantville, NY, 1979.

Bailey, L. R. *The A. B. Gray Report, A Survey of Route for Texas Western Railroad 1884*. Los Angeles: Westernlore Press, 1963.

Bierschwale, Margaret. *History of Mason County, Texas Through 1964*. Mason, TX: Premier Publishing Co., 1998.

Browning, James A. *Violence Was No Stranger*. Stillwater, OK: Barbed Wire Press, 1993.

_____. *The Bad Old Days, In and Around Sutton County 1889-1939*. Sutton County Historical Society, private printing.

Carroll, John M. *The Black Military Experience in the American West*. New York: Liveright Publishing Corporation, 1973.

Cox, Mike. *Red Rooster Country*. Hereford, TX: Pioneer Book Publishers, 1970.

Eaton, John. *Will Carver, Outlaw, San Angelo*. San Angelo, TX: Anchor Publishing Co., 1972.

_____. *A History of Edwards County, Rocksprings Woman's Club*. San Angelo, TX: Anchor Publishing Co., 1984.

Fisher, O. C. *The Speaker of Nubbin Ridge*. San Angelo, TX: The Talley Press, 1985.

_____. *It Occured In Kimble*. Houston, TX: Anson Jones Press, 1937.

Flemmons, Jerry. *Texas Siftings*. Fort Worth, TX: Texas Christian University Press, 1995.

Ford, John Salmon. *Rip Ford's Texas, Personal Narratives of the West*. Austin, TX: University of Texas Press, 1987.

Kinevan, Marcos. *Frontier Cavalryman, Lieutenant John Bigelow with the Buffalo Soldiers in Texas*. El Paso, TX: Texas Western Press, 1998.

Leckie, William H. *The Buffalo Soldiers, A Narrative of the Negro Cavalry in the West*. Norman, OK: University of Oklahoma Press, 1967.

Loomis, John A. *A Texas Ranchman, The Memoirs of John A. Loomis*. Chadron, NE, private printing, 1982.

McSwain, Ross. *Texas Sheep and Goat Raisers' Association, 1915-1995, A History of Service*. San Angelo, TX: Anchor Publishing Co., 1996.

_____. *Mason County Historical Book*. Mason County Historical Society, private printing, 1978.

_____. *Menard County History, An Anthology*. Menard County Historical Society. San Angelo, TX: Anchor Publishing Co., 1982.

O'Neal, Bill. *Encyclopedia of Western Gunfighters*, Norman, OK: University of Oklahoma Press, 1979.

Philips, Shine. *Big Spring, the Casual Biography of a Prairie Town*. Big Spring, TX: Private printing, 1942.

Pierce, N. H. *The Free State of Menard*. Menard, TX: Western Advertising Co., 1986.

The Texas Almanac, 200-2001, The Dallas Morning News.

Thompson, Cecilia. *History of Marfa and Presidio County, Vol. II, 1901-1946*. Austin, TX: Nortex Press, 1985.

Webb, Walter Prescott. *The Texas Ranger: A Century of Frontier Defense*. Austin, TX: University of Texas Press, 1993.

Welch, June Rayfield. *People and Places in the Texas Past*. Waco, TX: The Texian Press, 1974.

Williams, Jesse Wallace. *Old Texas Trails, 1716-1886*. Burnet, TX: Eakin Press, 1979.

Yarbrough, Jessie Newton. *A History of Coke County, Home of the Rabbit Twisters*. Robert Lee, TX. Private printing, 1979.

Magazines

Enchanted Rock Magazine, Vol. 5, No. 2, July-August 1998.

Enchanted Rock Magazine, Vol. 5, No. 3, September-October 1998.

Ranch and Rural Living Magazine, July 1995.

Ranch and Rural Living Magazine, June 2000.

Index